Memory

Wolfson College Lectures

Memory

History, Culture and the Mind

Edited by
Thomas Butler

Basil Blackwell

18558532
DLC

1-15-91

Copyright © Basil Blackwell Ltd 1989
First published 1989
Basil Blackwell Ltd
108 Cowley Road, Oxford, OX4 1JF, UK
Basil Blackwell Inc.
432 Park Avenue South, Suite 1503
New York, NY 10016, USA

British Library Cataloguing in Publication Data

Memory.
1. Culture. Influence of human memory
I. Butler, Thomas, 1929–
306
ISBN 0–631–16442–1

Library of Congress Cataloging in Publication Data

Memory/edited by Thomas Butler.
p. cm. — (Wolfson College lectures; 1988)
Includes index.
ISBN 0–631–16442–1
1. Memory. 2. Memory–Social aspects. 3. Memory–Political aspects.
I. Butler, Thomas, 1929–. II. Series.
BF371.M449 1989   88–28786
153.1′2–dc19   CIP

Typeset in 11 on 13pt Bembo
by Columns of Reading
Printed in Great Britain by TJ Press (Padstow) Ltd

Contents

Preface

The Wolfson College Lectures are given annually at Oxford during Hilary Term. Founded in 1970, the series of eight weekly lectures are open to the general public.

The 1988 lectures on 'Memory' reflect a continuing interest among the Wolfson community in matters of mind and culture. In the past there have been series on 'Structuralism' (1972), 'Mind and Language' (1974), 'Human Growth and Development' (1976), 'Literacy and the Written Word' (1984) and 'Functions of the Brain' (1985).

In proposing 'Memory' as the theme for the 1988 Wolfson College Lectures, I was motivated by a deep and longstanding concern that memory, the core of human culture, was endangered world-wide by governmental suppression and distortion, by techniques of disinformation, as well as by the general deterioration of public education.

I suggested to the organizing committee a programme of eight interconnected lectures designed to provide a progression from one topic to the next, with a view to their eventual publication as a book. After the proposal was accepted, scholars from the universities of Oxford, Cambridge, and London were consulted concerning the appropriate lecturers. We were concerned not so much with the reputation of a lecturer as with the quality of his writing and his direct involvement in some aspect of memory. For example, Alan Baddeley of Cambridge is not only one of the world's leading writers on memory (particularly on short-term or working memory), he has also been involved for years with the treatment of patients suffering memory loss or amnesia owing to trauma or disease. Bani Shorter, who followed him in the programme, is a practising London analyst, who knows first-hand about the role of our collective memory (the unconscious) in healing.

Shorter's exposition on myth and ritual leads directly into the next chapter, 'Memory and Oral Tradition'. For this we were fortunate to be able to invite a specialist from Yugoslavia, a country where the oral tradition is still alive. Krinka Vidaković Petrov's extensive research into Sephardic and Slavic folk song makes her contribution very rich indeed. Her essay is intended to dovetail with Peter Burke's on the relationship between social memory and history. Burke, a widely travelled Cambridge scholar with anthropological as well as historical training, discusses not only social memory but also social amnesia or the collective distortion of memory – a subject referred to earlier by Baddeley, on a more mundane level, in connection with opposing versions of a Dartmouth–Princeton football game.

Burke's chapter provides a bridge both to Geoffrey Hosking's insightful essay (he was the 1988 BBC Reith Lecturer), on the suppression and recent revival of memory in the USSR, and also to Patrick Wright's brilliant piece on heritage and the political questions that arise when a nation tries to decide what it wants to preserve and remember. (Hosking also has some interesting comments on the rise of a national heritage movement in the USSR.)

Jon Stallworthy's essay, finally, is about the relationship between memory and creativity, an essential topic. He shows how he and other poets suppress their conscious memory of their predecessors' poetry, while remembering it on a subliminal, creative level. Thus Stallworthy echoes and corroborates, in a very specific and delightful way, themes about remembering and forgetting that were earlier touched upon by Baddeley and others.

In addition to the interconnections provided by the structure of the programme itself, certain other, 'spiritual' affinities became apparent in the course of the series. For example, each lecturer seemed to share a consciousness of the crucial importance of our overall theme. I was impressed as well by the frequency with which *forgetting*, in its multiplicity of manifestations (distortion, suppression, amnesia, amnesty etc.), appeared inextricably entwined with memory. A further recurrent 'sub-theme' was *healing*. References to healing appear in almost every lecture, so that one almost suspects that the real (albeit unintended) purpose of this series was to advertise the many possibilities that memory offers for healing, on a collective as well as individual basis.

The Soviet Union is also mentioned in several lectures, as though she were never far from our minds, as an extreme example of the forced amnesia that has perverted the mentality of a large mass of the world's population. (Hosking treats the present-day revival of memory in the USSR, under Gorbachev, as the first stage in a healing process.) But lest we in the West become over confident or condescending towards our brothers and sisters to the East, we need only look at our own governments' current practices of disinformation, as a warning of what might be in store for us if we fail to respect the vital importance of preserving memory and truth.

As organizer of the 1988 Wolfson College Lectures, I should like to thank, first and foremost, Sir Raymond Hoffenberg, for his support, wisdom and practical advice. I also want to express my gratitude to Janet Walker, College Secretary, and Cynthia Flint for their administrative assistance, as well as to Nicholas Allen, Roger Booker, Jonathan Katz, Cecilia Dick and John Ashton for their ready counsel. Frank Kermode of the University of Cambridge kindly reviewed my preliminary programme, and gave some very helpful suggestions. Finally, a special word of thanks to my wife, Julia, for reading the manuscript and making valuable editorial comments, as well as to Peter Robinson for his encouragement and many excellent references on memory.

Thomas Butler
Wolfson College, Oxford

Acknowledgements

The editor, authors and publisher make grateful acknowledgement to the following for permission to reprint extracts from previously published material.

Heinrich Böll, Foreword to Eugenia Ginzburg, *Within the Whirlwind*: © Collins Publishers; Arnoldo Mondadori Editore.

T. S. Eliot, 'Little Gidding', from *Four Quartets*: © Faber and Faber; excerpt from 'Little Gidding' in *Four Quartets*, copyright 1943 by T. S. Eliot, renewed 1971 by Esme Valerie Eliot, reprinted by permission of Harcourt Brace Jovanovich, Inc.

Robert Frost, 'Stopping by Woods on a Snowy Evening', reprinted from *The Poetry of Robert Frost*, edited by Edward Connery Lathem: © the Estate of Robert Frost, Jonathan Cape Ltd; copyright 1923 by Holt, Rinehart and Winston and renewed 1951 by Robert Frost, reprinted by permission of Henry Holt and Company, Inc.

Seamus Heaney, 'Digging', from *Death of a Naturalist*, © Faber & Faber; from *Poems, 1965–1975*, copyright © 1966, 1980 by Seamus Heaney, reprinted by permission of Farrar, Straus and Giroux, Inc.

C. G. Jung, *Memories, Dreams, Reflections*, edited by Aniela Jaffé, translated by Richard and Clara Winston; © Collins Publishers; copyright Pantheon Books, a Division of Random House, Inc.

Philip Larkin, 'Talking in Bed', from *The Whitsun Weddings*: © Faber and Faber.

1

Memory: A Mixed Blessing
Thomas Butler

It seems appropriate to begin our exploration with a poem whose underlying theme is Memory – 'Digging' by Seamus Heaney:

Between my finger and my thumb
The squat pen rests; snug as a gun.

Under my window, a clean rasping sound
When the spade sinks into gravelly ground:
My father, digging. I look down

Till his straining rump among the flowerbeds
Bends low, comes up twenty years away
Stooping in rhythm through potato drills
Where he was digging.

The coarse boot nestled on the lug, the shaft
Against the inside knee was levered firmly.
He rooted out tall tops, buried the bright edge deep
To scatter new potatoes that we picked
Loving their cool hardness in our hands.

By God, the old man could handle a spade.
Just like his old man.

My grandfather cut more turf in a day
Than any other man on Toner's bog.
Once I carried him milk in a bottle
Corked sloppily with paper. He straightened up
To drink it, then fell to right away

Nicking and slicing neatly, heaving sods

Over his shoulder, going down and down
For the good turf. Digging.

The cold smell of potato mould, the squelch and slap
Of soggy peat, the curt cuts of an edge
Through living roots awaken in my head.
But I've no spade to follow men like them.

Between my finger and my thumb
The squat pen rests.
I'll dig with it.[1]

It is intriguing how images of ground and digging arise in connection with Memory. George Seferis's wonderful poem 'Mnimi' ('Memory')[2] comes to mind, as well as a strange parallel in the lives of a sixth-century Irish saint and a twelfth-century Tibetan saint, who were both fine poets. When Columba was walking toward the monastery of Bishop Etchen of Clonfad to be ordained he found the Bishop ploughing, and he thought it odd and unseemly that the man who was to ordain him should be ploughing a field. He wondered for a long time about that.[3] Likewise when the Tibetan Milarepa learns of a holy man who can teach him to achieve nirvana in one lifetime, he walks toward the guru's village and comes upon a corpulent man ploughing. He asks the stranger the way to the home of Marpa the Translator. The ploughman looks him over silently, pointing out the house; then he asks Milarepa if he first won't finish ploughing the field for him. After instructing him to 'dig it well', he gave him a jar of beer to keep his spirits up.[4]

When Milarepa finished his ploughing and finally reached Marpa's house, he was surprised to discover that the man who opened the door was the corpulent stranger, dressed now in monk's robes, albeit still sweating. It seems that Marpa had had a dream the night before, indicating that a very special disciple was coming his way, and in the morning he rushed out to plough the fields, not bothering to explain to his startled wife why he, a revered holy man and translator, should suddenly turn to ploughing.[5]

Perhaps Bishop Etchen of Clonfad had had the same presentiment regarding Columba – that a man of rare spiritual energy was coming his way. In both cases, the common wisdom that created these stories – whether they actually happened is not important – reminds us that we should have no preconceptions about likely sources of knowledge, and that spiritual transformation involves digging and turning over the soil.

I don't know when I first began to think about culture as Memory – I may have been 'digging' for quite a long time before I became aware of it. Various influences exerted their weight on my shovel, as I intend to show, but perhaps the very first glimmer of my theme came from reading the dissertation of my friend Father Russell Holmes, a discalced Carmelite and analyst. He had studied Jungian psychology in Zurich, and wrote his dissertation on 'Memory in the Works of St. John of the Cross and Teresa of Avila'. I had already begun to read Jung before I met Russell, including the autobiographical *Memories, Dreams, Reflections*, which had struck me with the force of revelation. I also read Jung's *Man and his Symbols*, as well as his work on alchemy,[6] and Aniela Jaffé's inspired *The Myth of Meaning*.[7] All these 'Jungian' works left me with the conviction that we don't come into the world with our minds a *tabula rasa*, but rather equipped with an inventory of archetypal patterns of thought and relationship that express themselves in common myths and folk tales. It became clear that such Jungian concepts as the archetypes can be grouped with other forms of belief in aprioristic knowledge, such as the ideas of Plato, Descartes, and Kant, and the linguistic theories of Chomsky.[8] The idea that we are born with some dim distillations of the experience, thought and spiritual achievements of our ancestors made as much sense to me as Darwin's theories of physical evolution. I began to conceive of man's 'history' as a spiritual evolution in which genetically transmitted archetypes were a primary means of intergenerational communication and growth.

Memory in Eastern Europe

The Slavic influences on my interest in Memory have been many, and so I suppose I should have been amused when asked by some colleagues: 'What's a nice Slavicist like you doing with *Memory*?' The answer is a long one, but I'll try to be brief. First I might mention my reading of Vladimir Dedijer's excellent historical study *The Road to Sarajevo*, wherein he analyses the background of the assassination of Archduke Ferdinand and his wife Sophie in 1914.[9] Dedijer traces the motivation for Gavrilo Princip's firing of the fatal shots that precipitated World War I to an event that occurred five hundred years earlier – the battle of Kosovo on 28 June 1389 when the flower of Serbian and Bosnian youth perished on the battlefield against the Turks.

This single loss doomed the Serbs to centuries of subjugation under the Ottoman Empire, but they derived one major satisfaction from the fateful battle. Their hero Miloš Obilić, pretending to surrender to Sultan Murad, ran the Sultan through with his sword. Murad's assassination raised regicide to one of the highest Serbian ethnic values, and constituted a revenge, a payment in advance for all the indignities to come at Turkish hands – the laws that prevented Serbs from having a horse of more than minimal value, from wearing a broad belt, or owning a weapon, from singing in groups, or building a church, or ringing a church bell.[10]

Serbs kept the memory of Kosovo alive in their oral traditions. After they won their autonomy, as the result of two uprisings early in the nineteenth century, they waited to unite with Turkish-held Bosnia. Austria's annexation of Bosnia in 1908 made a Serbian response inevitable. That the Archduke should choose St. Vitus's Day, the anniversary of the battle of Kosovo, to make his state visit to Sarajevo, tells us something about the blindness of imperialist powers, their disregard for national memory. Dedijer's well researched book shows that Memory, as transmitted through folk songs, epic poems, and oral traditions has the power to destroy empires, as water has the strength to crack stone. Men die for Memory, or one of her daughters, Poetry or Song.

The Russian writer Solzhenitsyn certainly helped shape my understanding of the importance of Memory to individual and national survival within a totalitarian system of government. Particularly illuminating in this respect was *One Day in the Life of*

Ivan Denisovich, which first appeared in 1962, and his later novels *The First Circle* and *Cancer Ward*.[11] Solzhenitsyn makes clear how important it was to his mental survival to express the truth about life in the Stalinist concentration camps. He found his true vocation as Russia's 'memory man', however, with his documentary *The Gulag Archipelago*. Today he lives in Cavendish, Vermont, where he operates a veritable 'memory factory', turning out the memoirs of Russians who lived from 1917 on. One feels that he is not motivated by revenge, but is looking beyond the present system in the USSR, and wants to set the record straight about the past.

A further Slavic influence on my interest in Memory was my friendship with Milovan Djilas, former Vice-President of the Yugoslav government, postwar ideologist, and then apostate and renegade, who wrote *The New Class*.[12] Djilas's disenchantment with the Communist Party really began in the early 1950s, when he wrote his 'Anatomy of a morality', about the young wife of a general, snubbed by the older members of the communist new class.[13] In defending the young woman Djilas may have been responding to some deeper call within himself.

It is intriguing to me, as an amateur 'Jungian', to see how for a male the rescue of the feminine can point the way to his own liberation, and in a symbolic sense to the liberation of a whole society. For example in the life of Columba, who made a revolutionary contribution to the spiritual foundations of Ireland and Scotland, there is a moment that is symbolic not only of his own future work, but also of the efforts of his followers to civilize their people. Once, when he was a young deacon, a girl came running toward him and his old mentor Gemman, chased by a rapist. Columba and Gemman threw their cloaks about the girl, but the man stabbed and killed her. Gemman's ensuing lament refers not only to the immediate tragedy, but also (because this whole scene is symbolically charged) to the very low status of women at that time in Ireland. 'For how long, holy boy, Columba, will God, the just judge, suffer this crime, and our dishonour, to go unavenged?'[14]

It was then that Columba showed that talent for levelling a curse possessed by the best of Irish saints, as he pronounced: 'In the same hour in which the soul of the girl whom he has slain ascends to heaven, let the soul of her murderer descend to hell!' Columba's biographer tells how the assailant dropped dead on the spot.[15] There is a similar story about Vasil Levski, the nineteenth-century Bulgarian patriot, who saved a fleeing girl by beating her Turkish assailant.[16] Strange, but Levski too had been a deacon, with a beautiful singing voice, like Columba.

Djilas had caused his share of pain and had behaved arrogantly during his days of power; yet he had plenty of time to repent in jail, serving nine out of ten years in Sremska Mitrovica, for condemning the Soviet invasion of Hungary, and for writing *Conversations with Stalin*.[17] When I first met him he had been out of jail several months, but he still had the prison pallor, and a kind of sheen that I associated with what William James calls a 'conversion experience'.[18] At the time (1967–8), I was in Yugoslavia with my family, on a Fulbright Professorship. I had been asked by the journal *Balkan Studies* to do a review of Djilas's *The Leper and Other Stories*, a book he had written in prison on toilet paper.[19] I knew that he lived around the corner from us in Belgrade, and one day as I was struggling with the idea that some of these stories were allegories about his former comrades, I decided to go and ask him. This seemed a bold thing to do – I was sure his house was watched, and how could I, a professor working on the history of the Serbo-Croatian literary language, explain my interest in talking with this outcast?

A woman came to the door. After I explained my purpose she disappeared for a few moments and returned, telling me to 'come back tomorrow'. The next day, after Djilas and I had our first cup of Turkish coffee, I got right to the point. I told him my theory about his stories. 'The "leper" – it's you, isn't it? And the one who betrays you, is that Dedijer?' (the same Dedijer who wrote *The Road to Sarajevo*). He denied it was Dedijer. We went through the stories one by one, and I took notes. Once he told me not to write down something he said. At another point, when his back was bothering him, he stood up and declaimed from *Paradise Lost*, which he had translated in jail.[20] 'I used the trochaic pentameter of our heroic epic – your English iambic sounds unnatural in Serbo-Croatian,' he said.

With respect to the theme of Memory, it is illuminating how Mnemosyne or one of the Muses (her daughters) comes to visit men in prison or exile; it's as though some men have to be rendered completely powerless over their environment before they will recognize the feminine or creative side that has been waiting for years to break through.

'Every man should spend some time in jail', Djilas said one day. Djilas was Memory – Yugoslav partisan memory, communist postwar macho euphoric memory, and disillusioned memory.

Once I told him that if I had been a communist, I would have been a Trotskyite – I had read Isaac Deutscher's two-volume glorification of the Russian revolutionary, who was exiled and later killed on Stalin's orders. 'Trotsky was a romantic and impractical,' he barked. I resented that. I knew what he was saying. 'With ideas like that, you wouldn't have lasted long in my outfit.'

Nadezhda Mandelstam's *Hope Against Hope*, concerning her life with the poet Osip Mandelstam in the Russia of the 1920s and 1930s, is the most profoundly moving piece of Russian memory I have read. She relates that she memorized thousands of lines of her husband's poetry in order to save them for the day when she could write them down. What makes her testimony overwhelming is her lack of vindictiveness, her feeling that victim and victimizer were mutually responsible. 'We were all the same, either sheep who went willingly to the slaughter, or respectful assistants to the executioners. Whichever role we played, we were uncannily submissive, stifling all our human instincts.' She resents intellectuals who say:

> You have to crack a few eggs if you want to make an omelette. When I see books by the [Louis] Aragons of this world, who are so keen to induce their countrymen to live as we do, I feel a duty to tell about my own experience. For the sake of what idea was it necessary to send those countless trainloads of prisoners, including the man who was so dear to me, to forced labor in Siberia? Mandelstam always said they knew what they were doing: the aim was to destroy not only people, but the intellect itself.[21]

Her testimony is so effective because she tells the story – her memory of what happened – from the ground level of everyday life, and with acceptance. She never once complains about her transition from the life of a comfortable, well-bred daughter of Russian professionals to a poet's wife with no income, living on handouts, with no apartment of their own. She was already healed of that searing experience, her husband dead thirty years, when she wrote *Hope Against Hope*. That may be why it has some strange essence of prophecy, of 'retrospective' prophecy, if such a thing can exist. Her reminiscences almost always search for meaning; we hear her thinking aloud as she tries to understand what went on, and we are reminded of Julia O'Faolain's aged nun Judith, who insists that Memory gives meaning to life.[22] Mandelstam had written a poem about Stalin in which he referred to him as 'the murderer and peasant-slayer'. The poem had never been published of course, but he had recited it to a dozen of his friends and that was enough to seal his doom. She writes: 'In choosing his manner of death, Mandelstam was counting on one remarkable feature of our leaders – their boundless, almost superstitious respect for poetry'.[23]

Another strong Slavic influence on my interest in Memory was Milan Kundera's *Book of Laughter and Forgetting*.[24] This émigré Czech writer is obsessed with the communist attempt to suppress memory in his native land. His heroine, Tamina, whose name may be a thinly disguised anagram of anima, tries to retrieve the eleven journals that she kept during her married life, because she wants to recapture the memory of her life with her dead husband. She represents the need of the present for grounding in the past. She also knows that 'she could never read her [journal] notes, if they had been read by someone else.' Here Kundera makes the point that intimate, personal memories have their full value only in a private sense; they are not for the public. Tamina's is an anti-artistic, anti-aesthetic viewpoint. She is not a writer.

In considering her attitude toward her notebooks, one understands why, even while fascinated, one feels something wrong, even sacrilegious in a book like Oliver Sacks's *The Man Who Mistook his Wife for a Hat*, which is a collection of stories (not case histories, in the strict sense) about actual patients of the neurologist Sacks.[25] We feel the same way in reading A. E. Hotchner's *Papa Hemingway*, which is Hotchner's record of the disintegration of the great writer toward the end of his career. His book is extremely fascinating, but seems to betray some personal trust, letting us too deeply into Hemingway's inner life. Do we have the right, even if our understanding is enlarged, to contemplate a great artist's degradation and folly, to watch his self-destruction unfold? Is knowledge always its own justification?

Kundera, to return to the Czech writer, contrasts Tamina's attempt to recapture Memory, with the Czech government's desire to destroy it. He calls Gustav Husak, the recent Czech president, 'the president of forgetting'. He quotes the historian Milan Hubl: 'the first step in liquidating a people is to erase its memory. Destroy its books, its culture, its history. . . . Before long the nation will forget what it is, and what it was.' Kundera touched me personally when he spoke of his father, who had a stroke and had lost his ability to talk. 'The silence of my father, whom all words eluded, the silence of the one hundred forty-five historians who have been forbidden to remember.' He writes: 'I understood the remorse Tamina felt. When my father died I had a bad case of it, too. I couldn't forgive myself for asking him so little, for knowing so little about him. That the external infinity escapes us, we accept with equanimity; the guilt over letting the second infinity escape follows us to the grave. While pondering the infinity of the stars, we ignore the infinity of our father.'[26]

Memory in the USA

When I left Yugoslavia in the fall of 1968, I travelled to Wisconsin to teach at the university in Madison. That was 'the year of the barricades'. Allan Bloom has written about this period of student unrest and violence in *The Closing of the American Mind*, which is a current best-seller in the USA.[27] Bloom was at Cornell when I arrived in Wisconsin; he was so upset by the student takeover at Ithaca in 1969 that he left for Toronto.

I had read about the student riots before leaving Yugoslavia, and had discussed them with Djilas. He said that nothing would come of them, because the students had 'no ideological basis'. He was right about the lack of a solid ideology, but the riots proved to have serious long-range consequences, not just in terms of the many young careers interrupted, but in the deterioration of the whole American educational system. We haven't yet recovered from the events of 1968–9, but the mushrooming readership of Bloom's book (over 500,000 copies sold!) would seem to indicate a genuine longing in the United States for that 'old time' education.

I remember watching the daily student gatherings, the late morning 'warm-ups' outside my office window – they never began early, because students were not going to classes. We teachers bent and relaxed our requirements, allowing for various types of make-ups, keeping our students on the books, hoping the situation would change; their enrolment was as important to our careers as to theirs. It was at Wisconsin that I saw the freshman English programme eviscerated as an administrative counterattack against the English graduate teaching assistants, who were among the ringleaders in the riots. Rightly or wrongly, I rationalized that these two groups, the rampaging know-nothing students and the stand-tough administrators, deserved each other. I was spared the flight of Allan Bloom and the heart attack he suffered in Toronto, but I'm not very proud of myself. As Nadezhda Mandelstam said: 'We were all in it together', and there wasn't much one could do but adapt. This was the period when all sorts of new specializations arose – Black Studies, courses in Black Language, Black Thought, Ecology (I sat on an ecology committee for a while, and liked it so much I considered a mid-career change), Folk Arts, Pottery – all kinds of pottery. I had a very good student in Bulgarian who graduated *summa cum laude*, while spending much of her time at the kiln.

I remember standing with a colleague on the seventh floor of the Van Hise building, called 'the Tower of Babel' because some thirty or forty languages were taught there, and watching the swirling crowd of students below, as they baited the red-neck Dane County Sheriff's deputies, who loved to come out and bash a few student heads after a night of drinking beer and brandy.

'If they only knew, if they only knew . . .' my colleague

sighed. He had escaped from Estonia in 1939 – the Russians had come in the front door and he had gone out the back. I suppose he thought he was watching the rise of a police state; but his words 'if they only knew' had a far different resonance for me than the one he intended, because I knew that they didn't know much of anything at all. I had children in the local schools and I saw what was happening on a day by day basis. New theories of education were cutting teacher–pupil contact in favour of so-called 'modular scheduling' and expensive media equipment. Children were getting less and less of 'the three R's' (especially writing), and were wandering about the corridors when they should have been in class. The growing illiteracy was manifested in the spelling mistakes the rebels made in their political graffiti, their frustration in the continual breaking of glass. A new kind of architecture was being introduced into public buildings – solid stone, slit windows, interior lighting, as in medieval fortresses. I remember writing in my journal 'a new Dark Ages is being born . . . the old mythology is dead . . . we need new myths'.

The myth of America's truthfulness in government was certainly dead. The lies and prevarication of the Johnson administration, continued by Nixon, destroyed our sense of identification with our government. Even when Johnson left the government, and even after the Watergate scandal destroyed Nixon, their techniques of governing lingered on, and we haven't got rid of them yet. What has all this to do with memory? Plenty! In the USA there are now 20,000,000 illiterates, and 20,000,000 more who are functional illiterates. When asked to colour in the United States on a map of the world, 25 per cent of high school graduates recently failed to do so. Without the ability to read, and without any sense of geographical orientation, much of our young population has no idea of their country, or its past, or the history of the various social movements that once made the United States strong – for example, the union movement. Without any respect for the genuine achievements of the past, without any social memory, how can these young people be expected to support a democratic society? It is such thoughts that have moved people like Bloom to call for a renaissance in American education.

One final comment on the state of Memory, East and West, before moving on to the nature of Memory. The Soviets and their cohorts have tried to suppress Memory and seem nonetheless to have revived it; we Americans have neglected Memory and it is dying as a result.

The grandeur of human Memory

The scientific description of the 'workings' of Memory, of our mnemonic system, seems to baffle even those who have devoted their lives to its study. In a recent article in *Scientific American*, entitled 'The anatomy of memory', M. Mishkin and T. Appenzeller write:

> Within the small volume of the human brain there is a system of memory, powerful enough to capture the image of a face in a single encounter, ample enough to store the experiences of a lifetime, and so versatile that the memory of a scene can summon associated recollections of sights, sounds, smells, tastes, tactile sensations, and emotion.

Mishkin and Appenzeller ask:

> How does this memory system work? Even defining memory is a struggle; introspection suggests a difference between knowing a face or a poem, and knowing a skill such as typing. Moreover the physical substrate of memory, the 100 billion or so nerve cells in the brain and their matted interconnections, is fantastically intricate.[28]

Just as awe-inspiring, and far more poetic, is Augustine's long rhapsody about Memory in his *Confessions*, of which I quote only a few lines.

> Great is this force of Memory, excessive great, O my God; a large and boundless chamber! Who ever sounded the depths thereof? A wonderful admiration surprises me, amazement seizes me upon this. And men go abroad to admire the heights of mountains, the mighty billows of the sea, the broad tides of rivers, the expanse of the ocean, and the circuits of the stars, and pass themselves by.[29]

When we read these last words we are reminded of Kundera's lament for having neglected the 'infinity' of his father's memory.

Perhaps one could conceive of Memory and its place in human culture in the terms that Carl Jung used to describe the relationship of the central archetype or the 'Self' to the overall Psyche: it is the core of the Psyche and the surrounding perimeter at the same time;[30] if we can accept this proposition (it evidently works in Jungian psychology), then perhaps we can also accept Memory as the core of culture and its surrounding ambiance as well. For Memory is not only what we personally experience, refine and retain (our 'core'), but also what we inherit from preceding generations, and pass on to the next. A truly global concept of Memory might include everything that ever happened – was ever seen, heard, said, felt, touched, smelled by every human being who ever lived, as well as by all other sensate beings, since animals also have memory. If we were to embrace the appropriate philosophical–religious system – Buddhism is the first to come to mind – we might even accept the idea that all the material of past memory still exists somewhere out there, in a great receptacle in the sky, the bin of memory, the Akaṣic record from which we all draw our karmic life plans.

In the realm of art, can we not say that speech, music, poetry are always memory events, and that when we speak we include the imprint of all the speech we have made in a lifetime, plus the speech experience of all those who have spoken our language before us? As the Irish playwright Brian Friel has said: 'It is not the literal past, the "facts" of history, that shape us, but images of the past, embodied in language.'[31] It also seems apparent that not only speech, but every artistic event, its creation and reception, involves Memory. John Sloboda writes:

> The way one hears music is crucially dependent upon what one can remember of past events in the music. A modulation to a new key is heard only if one remembers the previous key, a theme is heard as transformed only if one can remember the original version of which it is a transformation. . . . To perceive an event musically is to relate it to past events.[32]

The operations of Memory

I should like to move now from relatively 'global' conceptions of Memory, to the operations of individual, 'real-time' Memory. One can analyse personal Memory in terms of at least four stages: perception, processing, storage, and retrieval. It's obvious that few human beings have the ability to capture a complex sensory event in such a way that they can later reproduce it in all its complexity – the sights, sounds, smells, etc. There is almost always some abstraction attendant upon perception: one selects from an event according to various hierarchies of the senses (the visual is usually primary), in which our values also play a role. We have learned to process experience so quickly, that we usually are not even conscious of what we are doing. And we encode information according to some schema of which we are often unaware. If it be professional data we are more conscious of what we are doing, filing it with other material of the same category, updating when necessary. As for everyday life experiences, we most often have no filing system at all, leaving their later recollection to chance.

Emotion seems to be a good bonding agent for personal memories; except in extreme cases of fright or horror, an affective component can help both retention and retrieval. The Indian nonagenarian and Oxford resident, Nirad C. Chaudhuri, was recently asked how he could remember precise details of seventy and eighty years ago. For example, in his book *Thy Hand Great Anarch! India 1921–1952*, he writes: 'It was on 14 April, 1913, that I was going from Goalundo Ghat to Narayanganj in the river steamer Condor.' He describes the steamer as 'swinging around 24 degrees to port, as it went past the great pagoda of Rajabari . . . .'[33] An interviewer for the *Observer* asked Chaudhuri how he could explain this astonishing feat of memory – the ship's name, the precise date, the degrees to port. Chaudhuri answered: 'Memory is a product of life. . . . I don't memorize. It comes. I'm interested.'[34] Interest seems to imply emotion; he is emotionally committed to what he is doing at the time, and he evidently is undivided in his attention.

Retrieval is one of the more intriguing aspects of Memory. We know for example that if we file away information of 'interest', and rehearse it, chances are we can retain it for a lifetime. But what happens to all the other events that one never takes time to classify, that lie 'on top of the rubbish pile of life', as Borges writes in his story 'Funes el Memorioso' (Funes the Memorious)?[35] Is Aldous Huxley correct when he claims in *Eyeless in Gaza*, that Memory is a deck of snapshots shuffled and dealt by a lunatic?[36] And what are we to make of Borges' pessimistic appraisal of Memory in his poem 'Cambridge':

> Those odds and ends of memory are the only wealth
> that the rush of time leaves us.
> We are this chimerical museum of shifting forms
> this heap of broken mirrors.[37]

Finding himself on the wintry streets of Cambridge, Massachusetts, far from his sunny Argentina, Borges is emotionally drained. Nearly blind and without the support of friends and familiar surroundings, he thinks he has no memory – a conclusion which is obviously absurd in a man of such tremendous culture. For the moment he has no emotional weight with which to press the retrieval key, no sense of self, no identity. He is almost like Oliver Sacks's patient Jimmy, who suffers from Korsakoff's syndrome, of whom Sacks asks the nurses: 'Do you think he has any soul?' In other words, without retrieval does one have a soul?[38]

The matter of retrieval brings up interesting philosophical and religious questions. For example: God, shall we say, or Evolution has provided every individual with this huge mnemonic system with 100 billion cells, and a dual memory system, one old and one more recent, with some redundancy and distributed functions[39] – yet our retrieval network seems inferior, and to Huxley it is the work of a lunatic. Why? Did God do an imperfect job? Has the evolutionary process lagged in this area of our development? Or is Forgetting, i.e. the nonretrieval of most of the information that is processed in a lifetime, somehow a part of the plan?

Paul Fussell, in *The Great War and Modern Memory*, describes the poet Vernon Scannell going to Hardy's birthplace in Dorchester in June 1970, to read a speech in honour of Hardy's birthday. Scannell has reread much of Hardy's poetry for the occasion (including perhaps Hardy's 'Channel Firing'), and as he speaks he suddenly finds himself shifting to 'the thunderous invasion across the Channel' in which he himself took part twenty-six years before, almost to the day. Yet as he tries to recall the invasion he realizes that his mind has completely hidden from him the details of that frightening experience.[40] Fussell suggests: 'Perhaps his own psyche has providentially erased a host of memories that might do him harm.'[41] But judging from Sacks's descriptions of the traumatic or disease-induced triggering of 'lost' memories, there really may not be any erasure of our more awful memories – they are merely filed where we cannot get at them under normal conditions.[42]

There are of course exceptions to our general lack of recall of most of life's events. There are the 'idiot savants' mentioned by Sacks, who have tremendous eidetic memories. They seem to roll back the days of their lives at great speed, like some scroll, and if given a date thirty-five years ago, can tell us what day of the week it was and what the temperature was on that date, etc. Borges' Funes can even describe the cloud formations on a day long passed, but of course he is a hyperbolic, fictional creation. Borges makes an interesting comment on people like his Ireneo Funes; he wonders if they are too burdened with details to be able to generalize, and thus to think. The Russian neuro-psychologist Luria tells us that his mnemonist 'S' had a great problem learning to forget what he had once memorized, and that he was so overloaded with synaesthetic detail, forever struggling with the shapes and colours and smells of words, that it was nearly impossible for him to read literature or to think in abstract terms.[43] So nonretrieval, forgetting, even limited amnesia under acute stress seem to be an integral part of a normal intelligence, and are not necessarily signs of a faulty or imperfect system. Any proper study of Memory, then, has also to take into account *forgetting*. As a matter of fact, when I telephoned Yosef Yerushalmi, the author of the marvellous *Zakhor* (Hebrew for 'remember'),[44] to invite him to lecture on Jewish Memory, he declined, because of a book deadline. He added, mischievously, that he was 'a bit tired of Memory', and had just attended a conference on 'Forgetting' in Paris.

There are some memories that seem marginally painful, not so severe that we repress them, nor so dim that we lose them entirely. I remember one such memory connected with my brother. We had been close growing up, and had even slept in the same bed as small children. He followed me through school, always one year behind. But when we went to college, I didn't feel so close to him. He seemed to resent this, and dropped hints that college life had gone to my head. I always felt vaguely guilty about my treatment of him, but we never discussed it. Years later, driving through a town where I spent the summer with my wife and children, I went by a large store window and saw my reflection in the glass, and with a flash I understood why I had 'snubbed' my brother. He was so like me that he was my reflection – his softness, vulnerability, unsureness reminded me so much of myself it made me very uncomfortable. . . . So Memory, although painful, also brought healing in the end.

There are other, special kinds of recognition, connected with our system of encoding material for memory storage. For example, there is the encoding based on synecdoche, where a part stands for the whole. I remember that at my mother's wake an old but sturdy man thrust himself toward me. 'Do you know who I am?' I got ready to shake my head, but then I noticed a malevolent bit of a smile, a little curl in a corner of his mouth, and looking into his eyes for assurance I said: 'Martin . . . Martin Pendergast, our coal man!' I hadn't seen him for thirty years, but that one synecdochical trait, that memory trace, brought the whole Martin back to me.

And who has not been moved by the story of the two apostles who meet Christ after the Resurrection, on the road to Emmaus? The New Testament doesn't tell us why they don't recognize him, but the implication is that he has changed in physical appearance. Yet when they stop at the inn, and he breaks the bread at their meal, they immediately recognize him in that one action, and he disappears. They ask each other: 'Did not our heart burn within us, while he talked with us by the way?'[45]

Here the connection is made between emotion, the bonding agent, and Memory, and the whole impossible story somehow impresses us as credible, because it is consistent with the process of remembering.

In the Bulgarian folk song 'Krali Marko and the Three Soothsayers', a classic story of a male rite of passage, the three soothsayers come to King Vukašin's house on the third night after Marko's birth, to predict his future. The King overhears one of the women say: 'When he grows into a man, he will beat up his father.' Vukašin becomes frightened and puts the newborn Marko in a basket, setting him afloat on the Vardar River. A peasant adopts Marko, but even as a child he shows superhuman powers (or superbaby powers), killing the village sheep he is tending because he is too rough. Then, as a teenager he is asked to be a 'junior dever' (*po mlad dever*) for a princess who is to marry the Sixwinged Reljo. The devers are supposed to guard the bride, but when a monster comes out of the forest only Marko stays and fights, killing the dragon. He delivers the bride to the wedding celebration, and beats up all the guests who ran away, including his father, whom he naturally doesn't recognize. But something in the way Marko beats him leads the father to identify his son, and in this moment of synecdoche we have a beautiful instance of loving reconciliation, of Memory providing healing. Father and son get drunk together, and the party lasts for days, as wedding parties traditionally did in those parts.[46]

The art of Memory

In all such memory events we seem to be dealing with *invention*, the memory system abstracting one feature and filing it in such a way that under the proper emotional conditions it acts synecdochically, restoring the whole. Luria's mnemonist also used synecdoche, but purposely, as part of an artificial mnemonic system.[47]

The first developer of an artificial memory system was Simonides of Ceos (556–468 BC). An excellent poet, he was hired by the wealthy Scopas to recite an ode in his praise at a banquet. Scopas was not pleased with the poem, particularly the lavish praise Simonides accorded the mythical Dioscuri, Castor and Pollux. When it came time to pay the poet he gave him only half the agreed-upon fee, telling him to go to the Dioscuri for the rest. Just then a servant said there were two young men at the door, asking for Simonides. When he went outside the poet found no one, but at that very moment the roof of the banquet hall fell in, burying everyone.

The bodies of the guests were so mangled as to be unrecognizable even to their closest relatives, but Simonides was able to identify them because he could remember the exact layout of the hall, and who was sitting at what place. It was on the basis of this insight that he is said to have developed his system.[48] The artificial memory system prescribed the following: first one has to memorize the inside of a real or imaginary palace or other large building; within this memory palace one must designate loci (places) which can be rooms, corners, statues, etc. The palace should be well lit, and the loci should not be more than thirty feet apart. They should be learned in a series, so that one can start from any locus and work forwards or backwards. The same set of loci can be used again and again for remembering different bodies of material.

When one wants to memorize a new body of material, one invents new images for each locus of the memory palace, depositing with them the information one wants to remember; for example, at a statue of Poseidon one might hang an anchor, to remember a naval battle. The anonymous writer of the rhetorical treatise *Ad Herennium* states: 'The images we have placed on them for remembering one set of things fade and are effaced when we make no further use of them. But the loci remain in the memory, and can be used again and again, by placing another set of images for another set of materials.'[49]

With regard to the earlier designation of synecdoche as invention, it is instructive that the Roman rhetorician Quintilian uses the term in his summary of the system: 'We require, therefore, places (loci) either real or imaginary, [plus] images or simulacra, which must be invented.'[50] So the creation of these images would evidently relate to what we do in natural memory, when we take a slice of raw perception and transform or abstract it, inventing something absolutely new before filing it away.

The emotional factor in natural memory bonding was not overlooked by the artificial systems. The writer of *Ad Herennium* stressed that the choice of images was very important: they must be *imagines agentes* – striking images. 'They should arouse emotions and be close to the subject. . . . If we assign to them exceptional beauty, or singular ugliness; if we ornament some of them, as with crown or purple cloaks . . . or if we somehow disfigure them, as by introducing one stained with blood or smeared with red paint, the memory is stronger.'[51]

Such systems once enabled men to perform great mnemonic feats. Pliny, whose information cannot always be taken at face value, states in his *Natural History* that the Persian King Cyrus could give the names of all the men in his army, that Lucius Scipio knew the names of all the Roman people, and that Mithridates could give judgements in the twenty-two languages of his realm.[52] The elder Seneca, reflecting on the strength of his own memory when he was a young man, writes that he could repeat two thousand names in the same order given to him, and that he could take a line of poetry from each of 200 fellow students and recite them in reverse order.[53] Before leaving this discussion of artificial memory systems, I want to point out that Luria's 'S' struck on a similar system quite by accident. Taking for his 'memory palace' Gorky Street in Moscow, and starting at Majakovsky's statue, he deposited images and data at the doors of buildings he knew by heart, as he took his walk down memory lane. When he wanted to recall the information he merely repeated his stroll, stopping at each building along his way.[54]

An analogue of natural retrieval

I have a theory that the veneration of relics, itself a synecdochical memory ritual, may represent an analogue of the natural process of memory retrieval. The veneration of relics is not just a Christian custom, by the way; it is to be found in Tibet, and it existed in ancient Greece, as it does in Greece today. Classical sources tell us that the Athenians, after consulting an oracle, sent a search party to the island of Scyros to find the relics of Theseus.[55] We also know that the relics of St. John of Rila (d. AD 946), the spiritual founder of Bulgaria, were moved (the English term is 'translated') many times during the turbulent history of that country;[56] and here in England, once Lindisfarne had been abandoned to the Viking raiders, the relics of St. Cuthbert were translated from place to place, for eight years, until they found their permanent home in Durham.

Stories of the finding ('invention' is the technical term) of saints' relics, their translation, and display may cast light on an underlying analogue of the natural memory process. When their exact location is unknown an oracle is consulted, or in the Christian tradition an appropriately pious person has a dream in which an angel tells him where to look. St. Cyril (d. 869), the Slavic apostle who found in the Crimea the supposed relics of St. Clement, the third pope, dispenses in his account with the supernatural details common to such stories, but he does describe synaesthetic phenomena that attend the actual invention – the sweet smell and the luminescence of the bones. When the relics are washed in water everyone rushes to take samples of the liquid, because of its supposed healing properties; and we are reminded of the ultimate healing power of Memory.[57]

There are numerous descriptions of similar synaesthetic effects; for example at Canterbury, when the grave of Lawrence the second Archbishop was opened in the eleventh century, 'a mighty blast of fragrance swept through the whole monastery.'[58] Are such accounts fabrications? I doubt it. Whether psychically induced or not, the olfactory stimulation was probably accurately reported. Synaesthesia seems to be definitely connected with Memory, in both storage and retrieval, as extreme cases such as Luria's mnemonist make abundantly clear.[59]

If one accepts the possibility that the invention and translation of relics is a mime of the retrieval process, the analogy would seem to be with the finding of precious but often painfully accessed materials, with the bringing of strongly desired information to consciousness. What is especially curious is that in many accounts of relic inventions and translations, the ruler comes outside the castle or city to greet the relics, thus meeting the saint without the trappings of power. When St. Cyril brought the relics of St. Clement back to Cherson in AD 861, the chief administrator of the city (Nicephorus) came outside the walls with a candlelit procession to greet him. The same scene was repeated in AD 867, when Cyril brought Clement's relics to Rome, where he was met outside the city walls by Pope Hadrian II with a retinue of clergy. Likewise, when the relics of St. John Chrysostom were brought back to Constantinople from the place of his exile, in AD 438, the Emperor Theodosius II and his sister Pulcheria came outside the walls to meet them.[60] This would indicate, *inter alia*, that even sovereigns recognize that a nation ultimately traces its identity, its ethnic memory, to its spiritual lineage. In mnemonic terms, this part of the ritual may mean that the Ego (the ruler) recognizes that, when certain precious information has to be retrieved, it is powerless, and must wait for the spirit (psyche) to unearth it.[61]

Time and Memory

Now I should like to discuss the relationship of Time and Memory, and whether in a chronometrically oriented society, measuring time in abstract units called 'seconds', 'minutes', etc., we aid or hinder the process of Memory. Psychological or subjective time doesn't move at a regular pace, as everyone knows; some moments are timeless and so slow we can hear ourselves thinking, while others are so hectic and fast that 'hours' fly by like 'minutes'. How can we reproduce the essence of such events later in our minds, if we are recording them with an eye on our watch? The inner, affective content of important personal experiences seems vitiated by mindfulness of the clock!

Erich Auerbach, in *Mimesis*, has argued that the Old Testament is superior to Homer and Greek mythology, in that it established a chronological approach to history, whereas the Greeks were mainly interested in cycles of recurrence.[62] Such a position may need to be reexamined as it is becoming clear that our Western obsession with linear time holds disadvantages for personal Memory, and perhaps for spiritual and mental well-being. Yerushalmi, in *Zakhor*, muses about the continual writing of histories and histories of histories, and he states that History and Memory are not the same thing.[63] He wonders about the advantages of a cyclical, Greek approach to time. In a similar vein, Stephen Jay Gould in a recently published book underscored the necessity for a concept of Time which included both linear and cyclical elements.[64] During a talk I had with Frank Kermode in Oxford, in the winter of 1987, he brought up the subject of liturgical cycles and how they used to provide a framework for personal memories. One remembered that a particular thing happened just before Easter, or Palm Sunday, or Christmas. There was a cycle of holy days to which one could tack important events, but with the decline of religious customs Memory has faded as well. We don't normally look at the calendar on the day we say goodbye to someone, and forever remember the date. But a holy day, perhaps because of some affect traditionally associated with it, used to carry a special mnemonic bonding, one which helped us remember important personal experiences.

One final comment about the connection between Memory and Time: the Czech playwright Václav Havel, who was imprisoned for his activities as a founder of Charter 77, a group formed to oversee the observance of the Helsinki Accords, wrote an open letter to President Husak in 1975 in which he mentioned the loss of a sense of Time in their country, underlining its connection with Memory (and culture). He stated: 'Slowly but surely, we are losing the sense of time. We begin to forget what happened when, what came earlier and what later, and the feeling that it really doesn't matter overwhelms us.' On a more optimistic note, Havel told a recent interviewer for the *Times Literary Supplement* that as a result of the mushrooming of samizdat journals and the resurgence of independent cultural life, 'Time is beginning to become evident again, as if we were rejoining history.'[65]

Memory and Healing

I have already alluded to the connection between Memory and Healing. I would like now to clarify this relationship, and what it may convey for the future of mankind. As individuals we all may experience pain caused by others, and we may grow from the experience. There seems to be a dynamic of contrition and forgiveness between victimizer and victim, exemplified in the Jewish ritual of the Day of Atonement, one that cannot be overlooked in the healing process. But this dynamic doesn't seem to be recognized by some nations. One thinks first of the Holocaust. Who besides Jews, as well as the survivors of other holocausts, can really feel the pain caused by that horror? It was only when I went to Dachau and walked the ground of the camp that I began to understand the pain. I saw the pictures of Jewish musicians playing on the cart of a prisoner being taken to the gallows, a noose around his neck. Such *imagines agentes* will remain in my mind forever. But it was Lantzman's documentary *Shoah*, nine hours of film shot at ground level, that made me feel what he calls the 'incarnation' of the Jewish experience of the Holocaust.

Jews refuse to forget the Holocaust, or to forgive, said President Chaim Herzog during a 1987 visit to West Germany. Maybe this is an absolute position. Perhaps if enough Germans felt true compassion, the situation would be different. The German people have to relinquish their amnesia about World War II and to accept the responsibility for their crimes, as Richard von Weizsäcker, the President of West Germany, and the late Heinrich Böll, the Nobel Prize laureate, have pointed out time and again.[66] At Harvard University's Commencement in June 1987, in an address intended to mark the fortieth anniversary of the Marshall Plan, von Weizsäcker remembered the Holocaust: 'Millions of Jews had become the victims of an unprecedented crime. . . . We had witnessed what happens when the human mind is distorted by manic racism, terror and violence.'[67]

In France, the Klaus Barbie trial stirred up renewed misgivings about the role the French played in the extermination of Jews, a role whose memory cannot be dispelled by such films as *Adieu les enfants*, the story of a Catholic school director who is taken away to die with two Jewish children he has been hiding. The same is true for Austria, but more so. The controversy over

President Waldheim's activities during World War II has meant the reexamination of Austria's role in the death camps, where forty per cent of the workers are said to have been Austrian.[68]

Memory is playing its part in bringing the truth to light, not only concerning the Holocaust, but also in regard to Stalin's crimes against the people of the USSR and Poland. A special historical commission has been established to investigate the records of the Soviet Supreme Court. At a meeting at the Institute of State Archives in Moscow, in 1987, it was brought out that on one day in 1937 over 6200 prisoners were shot, and that more than 600,000 prisoners were actually registered as having been sent to the Gulag before 1937, the year the Purges are officially said to have begun.[69] An organization called *Pamyat'* – Memory – (which has unfortunate anti-Semitic tendencies) has been established in Moscow, with the aim of concentrating on the Russian past. In the United States we have recently acknowledged our crimes against the Nisei, loyal Japanese-Americans at the beginning of World War II, paying each survivor $20,000 as indemnification for their internment during the War.[70] Even in Australia the government is acknowledging the crimes that were committed against the Aborigines during the settlement of the country, but it doesn't seem to be in a hurry to recognize these atrocities in the official celebration of the bicentennial this year.

The many mentions of Memory throughout the world today – hardly a week goes by without a new article on the subject – make one think that we are experiencing a genuinely spontaneous movement of the heart or soul, a last-gasp, intuitive, nonpolitical effort to set the world on the track of peace and survival. It seems that this 'Memory Movement', or movement of Memory, has arisen to remind people everywhere that we need first to look at the past with a truly open mind and with as much piety as we can muster. Then we must 'reopen the old wounds', as Senator Robert Dole said at a recent meeting in Boston to commemorate the Armenian Massacres.[71] We must reopen the old wounds, so they can heal. Does anyone believe that the British victimization of the Irish happened so long ago that the Irish no longer carry the scars? Perhaps victims and victimizers everywhere can find a way to get together for honest, face to face discussions. We need a worldwide, religion-free Day of Atonement in which government officials and church hierarchy play no part. Just common people, attended by poets. Poets may write the new liturgies of reconciliation, since Poetry is close to Memory. And Memory not only causes pain, it heals.

Finally, the current revival of Memory may be pointing the way toward something beyond healing. A new myth for the future of mankind, one that doesn't see the world collapsing in an Atlantis-like nuclear disaster, one that offers hope. Toward this goal, Memory's rootedness in the ground of the Past and its traditional nourishment of Prophecy will be a great boon.

Let's begin the digging.

Notes

1 S. Heaney, *Selected Poems, 1965–1975*, London: Faber and Faber, 1980.
2 G. Seferis. *Collected Poems, 1924–1955*, London: Jonathan Cape, 1978, tr. E. Keeley and P. Sherrard. '. . . So I continued along the dark path/ and turned into my garden and dug and buried the reed/ And again I whispered: some morning the resurrection will come,/ dawn's light will blossom red as trees glow in spring,/ the sea will be born again, and the wave will fling forth Aphrodite.'
3 The story of Columba's encounter with Bishop Etchen does not appear in Adomnan's *Life of Columba* (late seventh century), but in *The Old Irish Life*, which was written down centuries later. See I. Finley, *Columba*, London: Victor Gollancz, 1979, p. 67.
4 There are two English translations of Rechung's *Life of Milarepa*, one by Evans-Wentz and Lama Kazi Dawa Samdup (*Tibet's Great Yogi Milarepa, A Biography From The Tibetan*, Oxford University Press, 1969), and the other by Lobsang P. Lhalungpa (*The Life of Milarepa*, Boston: Shambala, 1984). The scene in which Milarepa finds his future guru ploughing appears in part II, chapter 1.
5 Ibid.
6 C. G. Jung, *Memories, Dreams, Reflections*, ed. A. Jaffé, tr. R. and C. Winston, London: Collins, 1963. *Man and his Symbols*, London: Collins and Routledge & Kegan Paul, 1963; New York: Doubleday, 1964. *Psychology and Alchemy*, Collected Works, vol. 12, London: Routledge & Kegan Paul, 1953; New York: Pantheon, 1953.

7 A. Jaffé, *The Myth of Meaning*, New York: Putnam, 1971.

8 For a concise, pertinent discussion of Chomskian linguistics, see John Lyon's *Noam Chomsky*, New York: Viking (Modern Masters Series, ed. F. Kermode), 1970.

9 V. Dedijer, *The Road to Sarajevo*, London: MacGibbon and Kee, 1967.

10 My information on the 'kanun i raja', the Ottoman regulations for Christian and Jewish subjects, is derived from the Yugoslav novelist Ivo Andrić's doctoral dissertation at Graz: 'Die Entwicklung des geistigen Lebens in Bosnien unter der Einwirkung der turkischen Herrshaft', published in *Sveske zadužbine Ive Andrića*, god. 1, sv. 1. Belgrade, 1982, chapter III, pp. 70–3.

11 A. Solzhenitsyn, *Odin den' Ivana Denisovicha*, Moscow: Novy Mir, 1962. This was one of the major works published during Khruschev's 'thaw'. Later, after he was prevented from further publication in the USSR, Solzhenitsyn had to publish his novels abroad, for example *The First Circle* (*V kruge pervom*), New York: Harper & Row, 1968, and *The Cancer Ward* (*Rakovy korpus*), New York: Harper & Row, 1968), as well as *The Gulag Archipelago* (*Arxipelag Gulag*, I–II), New York: Harper & Row, 1973. GULAG is an acronym for 'Main Administration of Camps'.

12 M. Djilas, *The New Class: An Analysis of the Communist System*, New York: Harcourt Brace & Jovanovich, 1957.

13 M. Djilas, 'Anatomija jednoga morala', in *Nova Misao*, Belgrade, 1 Jan. 1954.

14 *Adomnan's Life of St. Columba*. eds. A. O. Anderson and M. O. Anderson, Edinburgh: Thomas Nelson & Sons, 1961, part II, chapter 25, pp. 383–5. The story of the murdered girl appears in *The Old Irish Life* as well (see Finlay, *Columba*, p. 61).

15 *Adomnan's Life of St. Columba*.

16 M. MacDermott, *The Apostle of Freedom: A Portrait of Vasil Levsky against a Background of Nineteenth Century Bulgaria*, London: George Allen & Unwin, 1967, p. 37.

17 M. Djilas, *Conversations with Stalin*, New York: Harcourt Brace & Jovanovich, 1962.

18 W. James, *The Varieties of Religious Experience: A Study in Human Nature*, London, New York: Longman, Green & Co., 1952 (the Gifford Lectures on Natural Religion, delivered at Edinburgh 1901–1902).

19 M. Djilas, *The Leper and Other Stories*, New York: Harcourt Brace & Jovanovich, 1964.

20 M. Djilas, *Izgubljeni raj* (*Paradise Lost*), New York: Harcourt Brace & Jovanovich, 1969. Djilas once told me that he identified with Lucifer. We had a good laugh about that.

21 N. Mandelstam, *Hope Against Hope*, London: Collins & Harvill, 1971, p. 363. The journal *Yunost'* has announced plans to publish N. Mandelstam's memoir.

22 Julia O'Faolain, *No Country for Young Men*, London: Penguin, 1980.

23 N. Mandelstam, ibid., p. 159.

24 M. Kundera, *The Book of Laughter and Forgetting*, tr. Michael Heim, London: Faber and Faber, 1980.

25 O. Sacks, *The Man Who Mistook his Wife for a Hat*, London: Duckworth, 1985.

26 M. Kundera, ibid., pp. 159–64.

27 A. Bloom, *The Closing of the American Mind: How Higher Education has Failed Democracy and Impoverished the Souls of Today's Students*, New York: Simon & Schuster, 1987.

28 M. Mishkin and T. Appenzeller, 'The anatomy of memory', in *Scientific American*, June 1987, pp. 80–9.

29 *The Confessions of Saint Augustine*, tr. E. B. Pusey, London: Dent, 1907, p. 213.

30 C. G. Jung, *Psychology and Alchemy*, Collected Works, vol. 12, p. 41.

31 Brian Friel, quoted in the *International Herald Tribune*, 2 Oct. 1987.

32 J. Sloboda, *The Musical Mind: The Cognitive Psychology of Music*, Oxford Psychology Series, no. 5, Clarendon Press, 1965, especially pp. 174–5.

33 N. C. Chaudhuri, *Thy Hand Great Anarch! India 1921–1952*, London: Chatto & Windus, 1987, p. 209.

34 The *Observer*, 29 Nov. 1987, pp. 21–2.

35 J. L. Borges, 'Funes el Memorioso', in *Ficciones*, London: Weidenfeld & Nicolson, 1962, pp. 99–106.

36 A. Huxley, *Eyeless in Gaza*, London: Chatto & Windus, 1969, p. 23: 'Somewhere in the mind a lunatic shuffled a pack of snapshots and dealt them out at random, shuffled once more and dealt them in a different order, again and again, indefinitely. There was no chronology.'

37 J. L. Borges, 'Cambridge', in *In Praise of Darkness (Poems)*, London: Allen Lane, 1969.

38 O. Sacks, ibid., p. 108.

39 M. Mishkin and T. Appenzeller, ibid., pp. 85–6.

40 P. Fussell, *The Great War and Modern Memory*, Oxford University Press, 1975, p. 334.

41 Ibid.
42 O.Sacks, ibid., part III, pp. 121–57, especially pp. 154–7.
43 A. Luria, *The Mind of a Mnemonist*, tr. Lynn Solotaroff, London: Jonathan Cape, 1969, pp. 112–36.
44 Y. Yerushalmi, *Zakhor. Jewish History and Jewish Memory*, Seattle: University of Washington, 1982.
45 Luke 24: 13–32.
46 'Marko Kraljević i tri narečnici', in *Bŭlgarska narodna poezija i proza, I, Junaški pesni*, ed. L. Bogdanova, Sofia: Bulgarski Pisatel, 1981, pp. 46–53.
47 A. Luria, ibid., pp. 42–3.
48 See F. A. Yates, *The Art of Memory*, London: Penguin, 1969.
49 Ibid., p. 23.
50 Ibid., p. 38.
51 Ibid., pp. 25–6.
52 Pliny, *Natural History*, bk. 7, ch. 24, tr. H. Rackham, Harvard University Press, Loeb Classical Library, 1947, II, pp. 563–5.
53 The elder Seneca, *Declamations (Controversiae) in Two Volumes*, tr. M. Winterbottom, Harvard University Press, 1974, I, bk. 1, preface 2.
54 A. Luria, ibid., pp. 32–3.
55 Plutarch's *Lives*, 'Theseus', ch. 36, mentions the invention and translation to Athens of what were claimed to be Theseus's bones, by Cimon in the fifth century BC.
56 John of Rila's extremely ascetic, secluded life has particularly attracted Bulgarians during periods of national crisis. Perhaps this is one reason why no less than eight hagiographic biographies have been written about him since the twelfth century. John's withdrawal from the world and his obstinate avoidance of contact with temporal powers holds appeal for Bulgarians to this day. Just as Djilas in jail felt moved to write a highly lyrical work on the Montenegrin cultural hero Njegoš, so the Bulgarian medievalist Ivan Dujčev composed a similarly lyrical reflection on John of Rila, during a time when not only his freedom, but his life was in jeopardy (*Rilskijŭt svetec i negovata obitel*, Sofia, 1947).
57 St. Cyril described the finding and translation of what he believed were Clement's bones in a special narrative, probably written originally in Greek and only later translated into Slavonic. My English translation of the rather garbled Slavonic version (the Greek is no longer extant) will appear in the forthcoming *Monumenta Bulgarica: A Bilingual Anthology of Bulgarian Texts*, to be published by Michigan Slavic Studies, Ann Arbor.

58 See A. Butler's *Lives of the Saints*, eds. H. Thurston and D. Attwater, London: Burns & Oates, 1956, I, p. 241. Butler quotes Abbot Wido, who translated the bones of Laurence of Canterbury in AD 1091.

59 A. Luria, ibid., pp. 27–8.

60 A. Butler, ibid., I, p. 182.

61 See A. Baddeley's *Working Memory*, Oxford Psychology Series, no. 11, Oxford University Press, 1986, p. 225, where he writes about the role of the 'Central Executive' in his theoretical working memory system. If one were to consider the invention, translation, display and/or enshrinement of relics as an analogue of retrieval, might not the king or local ruler who welcomes the translated relics be the equivalent of Baddeley's Central Executive?

62 E. Auerbach, *Mimesis: The Representation of Reality in Western Literature*, tr. W. R. Trask, Princeton University Press (2nd printing), 1968.

63 Y. Yerushalmi, *Zakhor*, chapter IV, pp. 81–103, especially pp. 94–6.

64 S. J. Gould, *Time's Arrow, Time's Cycle: Myth and Metaphor in the Discovery of Geological Time*, Harvard University Press, 1987, p. 16: 'Time's arrow is the intelligibility of distinct and irreversible events, while time's cycle is the intelligibility of timeless order and lawlike structure. We must have both.'

65 'Doing without Utopias: an interview with Václav Havel', in *TLS*, 23 Jan. 1987, pp. 81–3.

66 H. Böll, *Die Fähigkeit zu trauern. Schriften und Reden 1983–1985*, Bornheim–Merten: Lamuv. In many of his articles and speeches Böll criticizes his countrymen for their amnesia about the Holocaust and World War II.

67 Richard von Weizsäcker, President of the Federal Republic of Germany, in an address given at Harvard University's Commencement, 11 June 1987.

68 J. Miller, 'Erasing the past: Europe's amnesia about the Holocaust', in the *New York Times Magazine*, 16 Nov. 1986, p. 33. While denying any collective Austrian guilt, the Austrian President did finally apologize, on the eve of the fiftieth anniversary of the Anschluss, 'for the National Socialist crimes committed by Austrians'. Referring to the Holocaust, Waldheim said: 'These crimes cannot be explained or excused.' (The *Independent*, 11 March 1988, p. 10.)

69 Reported by the Soviet scholar Borisov at a meeting at the Institute of State Archives in Moscow in the spring of 1987. Borisov has been authorized to research the Supreme Court archives for

information on the purges. A key figure in the investigations of Stalin's crimes has been Dr Yuri Afanasyev, Director of the Institute, and brother of the Editor of *Pravda*. Since the reading of my lecture, the Russian revival of Memory has proceeded at such a pace under *glasnost'* that the Soviet administration, in recognition of the untruthfulness of Soviet history books, has absolved school-children from written history examinations until new textbooks can be prepared (reported by Rupert Cornwell in a front page article in the *Independent*, 11 June 1988.)

70 Massachusetts Congressman Barney Frank's bill for the indemni-fication of Nisei internment camp survivors was reported in the *International Herald Tribune*, 5 Oct. 1987. 'The nation needs the Bill more than the survivors,' stated Frank.

71 Senator Dole's speech was reported in the Boston *Globe*, 11 Oct. 1987.

2

The Psychology of Remembering and Forgetting

Alan Baddeley

As an experimental cognitive psychologist, I am interested in the scientific study of the psychology of memory. As such, my approach will be somewhat different from that of my fellow-authors in these essays since I shall be concentrating more on the question of what is memory, and rather less on its uses in culture and society. Nevertheless, I hope to persuade you that knowing something about the psychological basis of memory will be both interesting and useful in discussing its wider impact on society. In my overview, I will aim to convince you of three things, first of all that memory is important, secondly that it is a complex and rich capacity, and thirdly that despite its undoubted strengths it is eminently fallible.

The amount of scientific research carried out on memory in recent years has been massive, and inevitably I can give only a very partial and superficial account of some of that work. A more detailed version of my own view is given in *Your Memory: A User's Guide*,[1] while a good recent general survey of the study of memory breakdown is given in Alan Parkin's *Memory and Amnesia*.[2] I shall be saying nothing about the physical and biochemical basis of memory, an area of considerable current interest. Fortunately, however, this area is the topic of a special review edition of the journal *Trends in Neurosciences* published in April 1988. Finally, many aspects of memory are covered in the various sections of the recently published *Oxford Companion to the Mind*.[3]

No one would deny that memory is a faculty of some importance, but just how important? Perhaps the best way of gaining some insight into this is to consider the case of patients who have had the misfortune to become amnesic following brain damage. Any loss of neural tissue will tend to be reflected in slower learning and recall, but certain deficits can have an effect that is quite catastrophic. This was dramatically illustrated in a recent TV programme made by Jonathan Miller about Clive Wearing, a very intelligent and cultured man who became densely amnesic following encephalitis, a brain infection caused by the herpes simplex virus. Clive worked for the BBC and was an extremely talented musician. He was unconscious for many weeks, and was left with a desperately impaired capacity to remember new and ongoing information. Since he could not remember anything from more than a minute or two before, he was perpetually convinced that he had just recovered consciousness. A typical remark would be 'Consciousness has come to light since I was standing there . . . I was blind, deaf and dumb . . . everything has suddenly come back.' He was found on occasion with a notebook in front of him containing the statement 'Have just recovered consciousness 3.15 pm', with '3.15' crossed out and changed to '3.20', '3.25' and so forth. If his wife left the room for five minutes, on her return he would greet her as if he had not seen her for months, asking how long it was that he had been unconscious. In short, he lived in a perpetual present, which he described as 'like being dead – all the bloody time!'

He had rather better access to memories that occurred before his illness, but even here his memory was far from good. He had written a book on the early composer Lassus, and could answer a few very general questions on him, but could provide virtually no detail. When shown pictures of Cambridge where he had spent four years, he failed to recognize any of the scenes other than King's College Chapel. His general knowledge was likewise impoverished; he could not recall who had written Romeo and Juliet, although he could still talk in a lively and intelligent way on more general issues, such as the development of the role of the conductor in early music.

Amidst this desert of impaired memory, one capacity was marvellously preserved, namely his musical skills. His wife returned home one evening to find that he had been visited by his choir, and to see him conducting them with all his old skill through a complex choral piece. He could play the harpsichord and sing and to all intents and purposes appeared to have retained his marvellous musical facility. Despite this, however, his grossly impaired access to his own long-term past, and his incapacity to develop and build up an ongoing picture of experience make life for him 'a living hell'. A few minutes with Clive is enough to convince one of the enormous importance of memory. We all tend to complain that our memories are terrible; I hope to persuade you that far from being terrible the human memory system is superb, although fallible.

Memory systems and subsystems

I have written so far as though human memory were a single entity like the lungs or heart. It is much better considered as an alliance of several different systems, all of which have in common the capacity to take in information, store it and subsequently make it available. I shall begin by suggesting that memory can be divided into three broad categories, *sensory memory*, *working memory* and *long-term memory*. A diagram illustrating the relationship between the three is shown in figure 2.1. Information is assumed to initially be taken up by a series of sensory memory systems, shown on the left of figure 2.1. These are perhaps best considered as part of the processes of perception, and include a brief visual memory system sometimes known as *iconic memory*, and its auditory equivalent *echoic memory*. I shall not say more about them here other than that they play an integral part in our perception of the world. For example, if we had no iconic memory system we would perceive a film at the cinema as a series of still images interspersed with blank intervals, rather than as a continuously moving scene. Similarly, without echoic memory we would not hear a word, or indeed even a single tone as an entity. However, such systems probably do not play an important role in those aspects of memory that will concern the rest of the essays, and for that reason I shall now move on to talk about working memory.

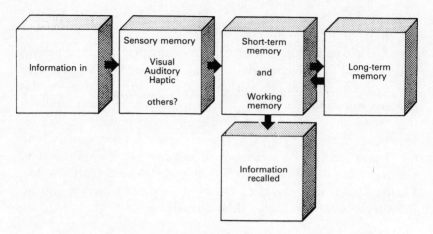

Figure 2.1 The flow of information through the memory system (adapted from Atkinson and Shiffrin, 1971)

Suppose I asked you to multiply 27 by 9. In order to perform this task you need to remember the 27, multiply the 7 by the 9, remember the 3, carry the 6 etc., etc., eventually coming up with a solution. In reaching that solution you will have to remember small amounts of information for short periods of time, subsequently discarding that information as it ceases to be useful. The system that performs this task of temporarily manipulating information is typically termed *working memory*. It is itself far from unitary, and figure 2.2 shows one conceptualization of the structure of working memory.

Working memory is assumed to comprise an attentional coordinating system known as the *Central Executive*, aided by a number of subsidiary slave systems of which two are illustrated, namely the *Visuo-spatial Sketchpad*, which is used for setting up and manipulating visual images, and the *Articulatory Loop*, a system that holds and utilizes inner speech.

Some feel for the operation of one's working memory can be gained from attempting the task of working out how many windows there are in your present home. Try it.

Most people attempt to do this task by forming a visual image of their house and then counting the windows either by imagining looking from outside or by walking through the house.

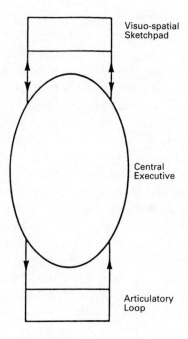

Figure 2.2 A simplified representation of the working memory model

The Visuo-spatial Sketchpad is the system used for setting up and manipulating the image, the Articulatory Loop is involved in the process of subvocal counting, while the whole strategy is organized and run by the Central Executive.

The system has been explored over the years using a number of approaches, including that of using a specific task to interfere with a particular part of the system. For example, a visuo-spatial task such as steering a car will interfere with the operation of the sketchpad, and vice versa. A particularly clear example of this occurred a few years ago when I attempted to drive a car along an American freeway at the same time as listening to an American football game on the radio. As I formed a more and more precise image of the game and its state, I found that the car weaved from side to side because of the interference between the two uses of my sketchpad. I hurriedly switched to a music programme.

A rather intriguing example of the use of the sketchpad came from a study of Japanese abacus experts. In Japan the use of the abacus for mental calculation is common, and practitioners become extremely skilled. With sufficient practice, the expert learns to dispense with the abacus altogether, relying apparently on a visual image. Using methods derived from the study of working memory, two Japanese psychologists, Hatano and Osawa,[4] showed that use of the sketchpad lay at the root of this skill, with the result that it could be disrupted by concurrent visuo-spatial, but not verbal activity.

In contrast, concurrent verbal activity can substantially interfere with the operation of the Articulatory Loop, which appears to comprise a system involving two components, a temporary auditory store, and a speech-based rehearsal process. It is possible to get some information about each of these in turn by trying the following short tests. In each case, read the sequence of words then look away and attempt to repeat them back; then check whether you were able to do this accurately and in the appropriate order. I will include sequences of both five items and six items in each case:

PEN	DAY	RIG	COW	HOT	
RIG	DAY	PEN	SUP	HOT	COW

Now try the next two:

MAP	CAN	MAX	MAD	CAP	
MAX	CAP	MAD	MAP	MAT	CAN

Most people find the MAD MAX set of words considerably harder than the others. The reason for this is that the memory store involved in temporarily holding strings of unrelated words is based on the phonological or sound characteristics of those words. Words that are similar in sound tend to be confused within this store, leading to poorer performance. Now try the next set:

HARM	WIT	BOND	TWICE	YIELD	
SOME	YIELD	BOND	TWICE	HARM	WIT

Now attempt the next set:

> ORGANIZATION   INDIVIDUAL   UNIVERSITY
> CONSIDERABLE   ASSOCIATION
>
> UNIVERSITY   INDIVIDUAL   ASSOCIATION
> OPPORTUNITY   ORGANIZATION   CONSIDERABLE

In this case, people usually find the short words considerably easier than the long ones. The reason here is that we maintain words in our temporary memory store by rehearsing them, subvocally saying them to ourselves. The system of rehearsal operates in real time, and consequently long words are rehearsed more slowly than short, allowing more fading of the memory trace between successive rehearsals.

If you were to stop yourself rehearsing by subvocally repeating some irrelevant words such as 'the' while reading and recalling the words, then you would find that your memory performance dropped substantially, but that you avoided both the similarity and the word-length effects. The reason for this is that you need subvocal rehearsal to feed the printed words into your auditory verbal store. If the subvocal rehearsal system is kept fully occupied repeating the word 'the', then the written material does not enter the store, and neither word-length nor similarity effects are found. Instead you rely on some alternative memory in terms of the visual or semantic characteristics of the words, a system that is rather less efficient than the phonological store for this type of material.

By using experiments of this kind we have been able to find out a good deal about the Articulatory Loop system. But what function does the system serve? This problem was made particularly acute by the discovery a few years ago of patients who have a specific deficit of short-term phonological storage.[5] Such patients appear to cope with life remarkably well, raising the awful thought that this system may be very useful for keeping experimental psychologists happy but of not much general significance. It might, as my colleague Jim Reason rather unkindly suggested, turn out to be 'nothing but a pimple on the face of cognition'. He might at least have referred to it as a 'beauty spot'.

In recent years we have been particularly concerned with this question and in particular have been interested in the cognitive abilities of the rare patients who are found to have a very specific deficit in this system. Close investigation shows that such patients do have problems in comprehending certain types of sentences, particularly those in which comprehension requires the listener to hold the surface characteristics of initial words across several intervening words. One example of such material is provided by self-embedded sentences such as 'The soldier whom the man had met on the train earlier in the week was wearing a large hat.' Such patients have difficulty in working out who was wearing the hat in these circumstances. Much more severe comprehension problems are occasionally found, and these we attribute to patients whose phonological storage capacity is particularly limited.[6]

However, a much more dramatic impairment was revealed in a recent study of such a patient in which we required her to learn phonologically novel items, such as would be the case if you were learning the vocabulary of a foreign language. Our patient proved quite incapable of learning even a single new vocabulary item when these were presented auditorily. When she was allowed to read the foreign words, she did show some learning, although her learning was by no means as good as that of control subjects matched for age and background. On the other hand, when required to learn pairs of familiar and meaningful words, her learning capacity proved quite normal.[7]

It appears then that the short-term phonological memory system is necessary for the long-term learning of novel verbal material. As such it should play an important role in a child's learning the vocabulary of his or her native language. A colleague, Susan Gathercole, and I have just been exploring this question using a sample of children who started school in Cambridge just over a year ago. We tested the short-term phonological memory of our children by requiring them to echo back spoken unfamiliar nonwords varying in length and complexity. We also tested their vocabulary, speaking a word and requiring them to point to a picture of the item denoted, and in addition measured their nonverbal intelligence and any reading skills they might have acquired. A year later we re-tested them using the same tasks.

When we analysed our results we found a close relationship between performance on the phonological memory task involving nonword repetition and vocabulary score. The relationship was still there when we allowed for other factors such as nonverbal intelligence and slight differences in age. One year later the relationship still held. Furthermore, the increase in vocabulary over the intervening year was predicted by their initial nonword repetition skills.[8] Our results suggest therefore that the short-term phonological store plays a crucial role in the long-term acquisition of language. So if the Articulatory Loop is a pimple on the face of cognition, then it is a rather important pimple!

There is also considerable evidence to suggest that phono-logical short-term memory is an important factor in learning to read.[9] Children who show particular and specific impaired reading development or dyslexia characteristically have very poor immediate verbal memory capacity. There is however a good deal of controversy as to whether poor verbal memory leads to poor reading development, or vice versa. There is certainly evidence that improvement in reading is followed by an increase in the capacity to perform phonological processing and memory tasks.[10] So which comes first? Since children presumably differ in their basic phonological memory capacity even before they start to read, we ourselves would wish to argue that this is fundamental. Our previously described study on children starting school in Cambridge should allow us to answer this in due course, but at present not enough of them have yet acquired the skills of reading for us to test our prediction. We should, however, be able to answer this question when we test our children for a third time in the autumn of 1988. In the meantime, we conclude that the short-term phonological store is important for the development of vocabulary, and may well be important for learning to read.

Long-term memory

I have so far concentrated almost exclusively on one aspect of working memory, the articulatory loop subsystem. Space availability forbids my going into similar detail about the rest of working memory; the interested reader is referred to my book *Working Memory*,[11] while I must move on to discuss that area of memory that is most closely associated with the remaining chapters in this book, namely long-term memory. Once again, it seems unlikely that this reflects a single unitary system, although there is still considerable disagreement as to how long-term memory should be fractionated. I will begin by discussing two theoretical distinctions that have proved influential in recent years, namely that between *semantic* and *episodic* memory, and that between *procedural* and *declarative* learning. I shall then go on to talk about two aspects of memory that are defined in terms of their real-world manifestations rather than their theoretical underpinning, namely *prospective* memory and *autobiographical* memory. This will be followed by an analysis of the points at which human memory is particularly vulnerable to bias and distortion.

In the early 1970s, the Canadian psychologist Endel Tulving emphasized a distinction between two aspects of memory that, as he points out, had long been implicit in the culture, but had not been explicitly acknowledged by experimental psychologists. He drew a distinction between episodic memory, by which he meant the conscious recollection of personally experienced events, and semantic memory or knowledge of the world.[12] An example of an episodic memory would be my recall of the experience of having breakfast this morning, or of meeting someone a year ago on holiday. Semantic memory on the other hand involves such factual knowledge as how many inches there are in a foot, what the capital of France is, or the fact that people often have cornflakes for breakfast.

There is no doubt that, as Tulving points out, there are very many differences between, for example, my memory of watching a rugby game on television yesterday afternoon, and my knowing that a rugby team comprises 15 players. What is, however, much less clear is whether these two examples reflect the operation of quite separate systems within the brain, as Tulving initially suggested, or whether they reflect the same system operating under very different conditions. This latter view might for example suggest that semantic memory represents the accumulation of information from many episodes or layers of experience, implying that, far from being a separate system, semantic memory is made up from multiple episodic memories.

A distinction that appears to have much stronger support is that between procedural and declarative learning. Procedural learning comprises the acquisition of skills, such as learning to type, whereby demonstration of learning is reflected in the more efficient performance of the skill. In this respect it is different from declarative learning, such as remembering going to a typing class, which is essentially the acquisition of new knowledge or experience. Procedural learning is knowing *how*; declarative learning is knowing *that*.

The most powerful evidence for such a distinction comes from studies of amnesic patients who have a major long-term memory deficit following brain damage. This can be produced by a number of causes including chronic alcoholism, brain damage due to head injury, or a stroke, or through a viral infection, as was the case with Clive Wearing, described earlier. Amnesic patients typically have great difficulty in recalling what they had for breakfast or where they are, or in remembering their way around the house or ward. Typically they would have normal language and normal working memory, and might have relatively a good memory for events occurring well before the onset of their illness or accident. However, they would show very poor performance on most standard tests of the memory laboratory such as learning lists of words, recalling complex patterns or recognizing previously presented faces or pictures.

Despite the general and often profound memory deficit shown, such patients typically show quite normal learning on a remarkably wide variety of other tasks. These range from classical conditioning, in which the patient learns to associate a sound with a puff of air and to close his or her eyes in anticipation, through motor skills such as learning to type or, for a pianist, learning a new tune, to perceptual skills. This last category might, for example, involve learning to read mirror-writing, or to find anomalies in complex pictures, where performance would speed up with practice, just as in people with normal memory. Similarly mastery of a range of puzzles and tasks can be acquired at a normal rate, including jigsaw puzzles, and even complex puzzles such as the Tower of Hanoi.

Although such amnesic patients show very poor learning of words, there are certain conditions in which their verbal learning also proves to be normal. One of the most striking of these is one in which the subject is given a series of words to learn, and is then cued to remember them by being presented with a fragment of the original. For example, one of the words might be PERFUME. If tested by recognition, with the patient required to say which of a number of words had been presented before, then the amnesic patient performs very poorly. However, given the initial letters PER and asked to come up with the first word that comes to mind, then the amnesic patient will perform extremely well, showing just as much advantage from previously having seen the target word as a normal subject asked to perform in this way.

What all these examples have in common is that they allow the patient to demonstrate learning, without the need for conscious awareness of the learning process. Typically, indeed, amnesic patients will deny having encountered the task before, at the same time as they are showing perfectly normal learning. This therefore seems to argue for two separate aspects of learning, one involving the capacity to reflect on prior experience, a capacity that is grossly impaired in amnesic patients. The second involves the apparently automatic display of learning in tasks where recollection of the learning event is unnecessary; such procedural learning appears to be intact in densely amnesic patients.

Long-term memory therefore appears to involve two separate types of learning: declarative and procedural. Declarative learning appears to be associated with conscious recollection of the past, and its adequate functioning appears to be disrupted by damage to a number of cortical and subcortical structures including the temporal lobes, the hippocampi and the mamillary bodies. In contrast, damage to these areas does not appear to prevent the more automatic process of procedural learning. Whether procedural learning will ultimately prove to be a single unitary system, or whether procedural tasks merely have in common the fact that they do not require conscious recollection, is still a very open question.

Prospective memory: remembering to remember

The psychology of memory succeeded in separating itself from the more speculative philosophical approach to memory by dint of simplification. In particular, the father of research on human memory, the nineteenth-century German psychologist Herman Ebbinghaus, was the first person to demonstrate the possibility of quantitative exploration of the characteristics of human memory. He did so by reducing the complexities of real-world memory to the simple learning by rote of meaningless verbal material, teaching himself to recite long sequences of invented nonwords such as TOV, ZIL and KIJ, and carefully measuring those factors that influenced rate of learning and forgetting.

The Ebbinghaus tradition played an important role in the development of the psychology of memory, but it has the weakness that it tends to concentrate too heavily on simplified and apparently soluble problems, and to neglect the richness of memory in the world at large. There have in recent years been increasing efforts to link the memory laboratory and the world, typically by taking laboratory phenomena and looking for their real-world implications, as for example in the case of our studies on the role of the articulatory loop system of working memory. Equally important, however, is a willingness to take aspects of memory that are important in everyday life, and ask what are the implications of these for current theories of memory. I will briefly describe two such areas, one concerned with *prospective memory*, or remembering to do things, while the other, *autobiographical memory*, refers to our capacity to remember the events of our own lives.

If someone tells you that they have a terrible memory, it typically implies that they are prone to making memory lapses such as forgetting appointments or failing to remember where they have left things around the house. How is this type of memory related to the system studied by psychologists in the laboratory? A colleague, Arnold Wilkins, and I became interested in the problem of studying this a few years ago.[13] We wanted to simulate the task of remembering to take pills four times a day, and in order to do so Arnold invented a simple but ingenious device. This comprised a light-tight box containing a digital watch and a film. When a button on the box was pressed, the dial of the watch was illuminated and the time registered on the film, which was then moved on. The subjects were instructed to press the button at four specified times each day for a period of a week. We carefully selected two groups of subjects, one that we knew to be very good at remembering lists of words, and one that was rather poor at this task. We were interested in whether the two groups would differ in remembering to 'take their pills'.

We found that significant differences between the two groups did indeed occur, but that the subjects who were particularly good at remembering words were the least punctual and accurate in pressing the button, a phenomenon we subsequently labelled the absent-minded professor effect. It seems likely that remembering to do things at the right time depends on things other than having a good general memory. There is, for example, evidence that elderly people become significantly poorer at learning new material, but report fewer memory lapses. While some of this apparent improvement with age may simply be due to the fact that the elderly are more likely to forget their memory lapses before they are asked to report them, other evidence suggests that this is not the only cause. In one study, for example, where subjects were instructed to telephone the experimenter at a specified time in the future, the elderly were consistently more reliable and accurate than the young.[14] The reason for this is probably that they have learnt to organize their lives in a much more structured way than the young, hence compensating for a memory system that is perhaps not quite what it used to be.

Does remembering to do things therefore depend on an entirely different system from the rest of memory? We now know that this is not the case. In order to obtain a good and reliable estimate of everyday memory problems, Barbara Wilson, a colleague who at that time was working at the Rivermead Rehabilitation Centre in Oxford, came up with a novel kind of memory test. This involved requiring the patient to perform a number of tasks, each of which attempted to test objectively a situation in which patients report a tendency to memory lapses. For example, he or she would be required to learn the name of a person in a photograph, to learn a new route, to memorize and subsequently recognize photographs of new people, and to indicate orientation in time and place. In addition, a number of tests of prospective memory were included; for example the patient was asked for some small personal item, such as a comb, which was secreted in a drawer, and was given the instruction that he or she should remember to ask for it at the end of the test. [15]

The Rivermead Behavioural Memory Test was subsequently validated using a large number of patients attending the Rehabilitation Centre. It proved to be a good measure of everyday memory, correlating quite highly ($r = 0.75$) with the observation of memory lapses in the patients made by therapists over many hours of treatment. It also proved to be the case that prospective memory was impaired in those patients who performed poorly on other tests of memory, including such traditional tasks as learning lists of words and recalling complex figures. [16] Indeed, a subsequent study which applied the test to the normal elderly showed that those items that tested prospective memory were particularly susceptible to the effects of age. [17]

In conclusion, then, it appears that remembering to do things does depend on the same system as is reflected in standard laboratory memory tasks. In addition, however, it probably depends rather crucially both on the way in which one organizes one's life, and on how important it is to remember that particular feature. Forgetting an appointment, birthday or anniversary can be hurtful in a way that forgetting an address or telephone number is not; the reason is that forgetting to do things certainly in part reflects the fallibility of our memory, but it also reflects the importance that we place on the event in question.

People often claim of an elderly relative that they have a marvellous memory. When questioned further, this usually means not that they make no errors of prospective memory, but rather that they appear to show an amazing capacity to recollect the events from their earlier life, sometimes prompting the speculation that age somehow enhances early memories. On the whole the evidence does not support this view; the elderly tend to be poorer at recalling both recent and distant events. They are, however, likely to spend rather more time reminiscing about the past, and hence to revive and go over certain old memories in a way that makes them perhaps more accessible than they were during the middle years when attention was probably focused more firmly on the present and the future.

Autobiographical memory

The systematic study of autobiographical memory began over a century ago with the work of Sir Francis Galton,[18] but was then neglected until a relatively recent revival of interest. The reason for its neglect is probably the complexity of the topic, with the difficulty of turning rich but potentially unreliable information into readily quantifiable and verifiable results.

In my own case, the development of interest in autobiographical memory stemmed from a discovery that amnesic patients who were otherwise very similar might differ quite markedly in their capacity to recollect their own earlier life. In order to explore this further, we adopted the technique originally pioneered by Galton, whereby the patient is given a word such as *river*, and asked to try to recollect some specific personally experienced event that is associated with a river. The resulting memory is then classified as to its richness, specificity and reliability.

Using these criteria, we found that patients tended to fall into one of three categories. Some patients appeared to have relatively normal memories of the period before their illness, whereas others appeared to view their past as if through a dense cloud. Yet a third group proved to be particularly intriguing since they gave what appeared to be rich and detailed recollections which subsequently proved to be quite fictitious. Such confabulating patients were typically those with severe damage to the frontal lobes, coupled with an amnesic deficit. The frontal lobes appear to be responsible among other things for the control of behaviour, for the operation of the central executive component of working memory for example, and a deficit in this system appears to lead to confabulation. Such confabulation is worth discussing in rather more detail since it has interesting impli-cations for the veracity of autobiographical memory in normal subjects, raising as it does the question of how we separate truth, or approximate truth, from fantasy in recalling our own past.

The confabulated memory sometimes has an amusing and almost surrealistic character as in the following recollection produced by a patient, NW, who in response to the cue word *make* previously described making a gramophone turntable at school. On being re-tested on a later occasion he did not report this, and I attempted to prompt him by mentioning that he had described something made at school, whereupon he produced the following:

ADB Can you think of anything you made at school that is striking?

NW An Australian wombat.

ADB An Australian wombat?

NW Ashtray, something different.

ADB That does sound different. How do you make an Australian wombat ashtray?

NW Get a piece of wood, let your imagination go . . .

ADB Did you make anything else that you can think of, a bit more conventional?

NW No I don't think so; I made a daffodil, again in wood. That was all to do with the school play.

ADB How was it to do with the school play?

NW There was a bowl of fruit and flowers which had to be given to the queen, Queen Diadem. All the various people had to make a flower. We were told to make something out of wood; I happened to be asked to make the daffodil, one of the easier pieces.

As this particular recollection might suggest, one occasionally wonders whether the patient is not simply teasing the experimenter. I think not, for a number of reasons. First of all, such confabulations are by no means limited to discussions with psychologists. In the case of one of our patients, RJ, for example, his wife reported that when he was home one weekend he turned to her in bed and asked 'Why do you keep telling people we are married?' 'But we are married, we've got three children,' retorted his wife. 'That doesn't necessarily mean we're married.' Whereupon his wife got out of bed and produced the wedding photographs, in response to which her husband commented 'Well that chap does look like me, but it's not!'

The same patient also would hold with considerable stubbornness to his often misguided memory, insisting for example that he should be in occupational therapy next and not physiotherapy, or that his luggage had been stored in a loft, and climbing on a toilet seat in order to access the non-existent loft. As the last incident implies, he was certainly willing to act on his confabulations. On one occasion he was found wheeling a fellow patient down the road. When stopped he reported that he was taking his friend to show him the sewage works that he was working on. He had indeed been involved in building a sewage works as a civil engineer, but that was many years ago and many miles away.

So why does confabulation occur? We suspect that it requires a combination of two things, first of all an impaired or clouded autobiographical memory, and secondly a deficit in that aspect of the central executive of working memory that is necessary for controlling and evaluating behaviour. We believe that given the difficult task of retrieving a specific memory associated with a highly constrained cue word, the patient with a deficit in the central executive is unable to access a genuine memory. What he produces instead is some form of association which he accepts and elaborates. Without the adequate control of the process of retrieval, what is produced is something rather closer to a free association or a dream.

Normal subjects do not on the whole confabulate, partly because they have better access to their memory traces, and so have less need to invent memories, and partly because they have a much better checking mechanism for the plausibility of whatever their memory might produce. I suspect, however, that this is a matter of degree rather than an absolute difference. On the whole we do not go in for florid confabulation, but in subtler ways our memories can be highly unreliable, and I would like to conclude by reviewing some of the ways in which our memories are fallible.

Bias and emotion

Memories are systems for storing information, and as such are required to do three things: to take in the necessary information, to store it, and to retrieve it at the appropriate time. Human memory is potentially fallible at each of these points.

Consider first the way in which information is registered in memory. This of course depends on attention. If we do not attend to something, then we are very unlikely to remember it, despite the claims to the contrary of those who try to sell courses of sleep learning and other allegedly painless roads to knowledge. What we attend to is determined by our interests and prejudices, as was demonstrated many years ago by the Princeton social psychologists Hastorf and Cantrill.[19] They describe a football game between Dartmouth and Princeton that aroused passionate commitment on both sides. Princeton had a particularly talented quarterback who was injured early in the game, a game that subsequently became increasingly violent. Hastorf and Cantrill report the account of the game given in the Princeton and Dartmouth college newspapers. It is not hard to guess which newspaper is which.

> This observer has never seen quite such a disgusting exhibit of so-called 'sport'. Both teams were guilty but the blame must be laid primarily on Dartmouth's doorstep. Princeton, obviously the better team, had no reason to rough up Dartmouth. Looking at the situation rationally, we don't see why the Indians should make a deliberate attempt to cripple Dick Kazmaier or any other Princeton player. The Dartmouth psychology, however, is not rational itself.

However, the Dartmouth–Princeton game set the stage for the other type of dirty football. A type which may be termed as an unjustifiable accusation. Dick Kazmaier was injured early in the game . . . after this incident [the coach] instilled the old see-what-they-did-go-get-them attitude into his players. His talk got results. Gene Howard and Jim Millar [from Dartmouth] were both injured. Both had dropped back to pass, had passed, and were standing unprotected in the back field. Result: one bad leg and one leg broken. The game was rough and did get a bit out of hand in the third quarter. Yet most of the roughing penalties were called against Princeton.

But is this a memory effect? Hastorf and Cantrill investigated this by showing a film of the game to both Dartmouth and Princeton students, asking them to note when they observed a piece of foul play. In the case of Dartmouth infringements there was a clear difference between the two with Princeton students reporting a mean of 9.8 while the Dartmouth students reported 4.3.

The tendency to see and remember things from an egocentric viewpoint is of course not limited to situations involving conflict. A particularly intriguing example of rather more subtle effects of bias was shown in Neisser's[20] analysis of the testimony given by John Dean in the Watergate investigation. You may recall that the press were so struck by Dean's apparent capacity to remember specific conversations in great detail, that they dubbed him 'the man with the tape recorder memory'. When the actual tape recordings of the conversations subsequently became available it proved possible to check the accuracy of this claim.

In terms of the gist of the conversations, Dean's recollection was in fact reasonably accurate, but the detail showed considerable distortion. The nature of the distortion was interesting in that it typically resulted in Dean's own role being perceived as more important and more central than it was, an egocentric bias that I suspect most of us would show in a similar situation.

To return to our students watching the football game; bias in their viewpoint was clearly one factor, but another could well have been the degree of emotion generated by the 'big game'. What role does emotion play in memory? This is of course a point of some importance in the case of a witness recalling a violent crime.

A short while ago I was telephoned one Sunday evening by a caller who introduced himself as a detective from the San Diego Police Force. He was involved in the investigation of a multiple murderer who had the unsavoury habit of slashing his victims' throats. Six people had been killed, but a seventh survived and identified someone as the attacker. What, I was asked, would be the influence of extreme emotion on the victim's memory?

The answer is that, on the whole, introducing emotion tends to reduce the accuracy with which an eyewitness can remember a crime; it does not apparently imprint the incident indelibly on the memory, as one might guess. However, when asked if the level of emotion generated in the experimental studies was equivalent to the level that the San Diego slasher's victim was likely to have experienced, I had to admit that it was certainly not. Even the most dedicated experimental psychologists do not, I am happy to say, threaten to cut their subjects' throats, even in the interests of science.

It is clear then that bias and emotion can both cause distortion in what gets into memory. Suppose, however, that information does get into memory, what factors will influence the durability of memory storage? While information on speed of forgetting is still surprisingly sparse, the evidence on the whole suggests that differential rates of forgetting for different kinds of material is not very common. Needless to say, increased forgetting can be produced by brain damage, or by the more temporary effects of a blow on the head. But the ability to remember an incident can also be substantially impaired by presenting interfering or misleading information.

This again has obvious practical implications in the case of eyewitness testimony, and there has in recent years been a great deal of interest in the distortions of memory that can be produced when leading questions are inserted into the subsequent interrogation of the witness. For example, choice of words can bias the subject's subsequent recall. In one study, Loftus and Palmer[21] showed subjects a film of a car crash, and subsequently questioned them about various details. One question concerned the speed at which one car was moving when it hit the other. Some subjects were asked 'About how fast were the cars going when they hit each other?', while for others the word 'hit' was replaced with 'contacted', 'bumped', 'collided' or 'smashed'. Estimated speeds ranged from 31.8 miles per hour for 'contacted' to 40.8 for 'smashed'. When questioned a week later as to whether any glass had been broken, subjects who had encountered the word 'smashed' were significantly more likely to report, falsely, that glass had been broken.

In other studies, Loftus and her collaborators were able to change subjects' views on a whole range of features of observed incidents, including the colour of cars, and whether a Stop sign or a Yield sign was present, while in another study many subjects were induced to report the presence of a non-existent barn. In all these cases, the distorted information was introduced parenthetically during an earlier question, and only subsequently probed directly. Subjects do not appear to be aware of the source of their mistake, and allowing them a second guess, or paying them a substantial amount for making the correct response, had no effect on the bias.

At this point, Loftus began to conclude that a permanent modification had been made in the underlying memory trace, with the old information destroyed by the new. However, as she fully realized, failure to find the old trace did not necessarily mean that it had been destroyed, rather than simply made unavailable.

Indeed a subsequent study by Bekerian and Bowers[22] showed that the old trace had survived, and given an appropriate method of retrieval it could be accessed. The studies by Loftus typically involved questioning the subject about the incident in a relatively unstructured way. Bekerian and Bowers showed that if the questions followed the order of the events in strict sequence, then subjects were able to access the original information, and to escape from the bias introduced by subsequent questions. In short, the Loftus effect is not due to destruction of the memory trace but is due to interfering with its retrieval.

Retrieval

Before discussing further potential distortions in human memory that occur at the retrieval stage, it is perhaps worth describing the process of retrieval in somewhat more detail. One way of doing so is to draw an analogy between human memory and an inanimate storage system such as a library. A library could operate merely as a passive storehouse in which books were piled up as they arrived. Such a system would, however, not be very easy to use unless one virtually always needed one of the last few books to have entered the system. If one needed to access books on the basis of subject, then it is of course essential to have a subject catalogue, and if a book has not been correctly catalogued when it came in, then retrieving it is going to be a very difficult and haphazard process. The secret of a good memory, as of a good library, is that of organization; good learning typically goes with the systematic encoding of incoming material, integrating and relating it to what is already known.

Suppose, however, that one has encoded the material appropriately; what is the process whereby one calls up the right memory at the right time? While we are still some way from fully understanding the retrieval process, one feature is captured by what Tulving has termed *encoding specificity*. On the whole, we access a piece of information by feeding in a fragment of what we wish to recall; the more accurate and complete the fragment, the better the chance of retrieval.

One aspect of this that has been known for centuries is the phenomenon of *context dependency*, the tendency for what is learnt in one situation to be best recalled in that situation. The philosopher John Locke recounts the tale of a young man who learnt to dance. His lessons always occurred in an attic that had a large trunk in it. Locke reports that while the young man could dance extremely well in the attic, if the trunk was removed he was no longer able to remember the steps.

How good is the scientific evidence for such context dependency? While there are not too many experiments on memory for dancing, there certainly is evidence that memory may be influenced by context. For example a colleague, Duncan

Godden, and I studied memory in deep-sea divers. We had our divers learn lists of words either on the beach, or 10 feet under the sea, and subsequently recall them in the wet or the dry environment. What we found was that regardless of where they learnt the words, they remembered about 40 per cent less when they were trying to recall them in the opposite environment.

Such a result could have rather dramatic implications; would all our students show dramatically good memory if their examinations were held in the lecture theatre, and will they forget everything once they have left the University? While the latter suggestions may indeed be true, it is probably not a result of context dependency, since effects as large as those we obtained occur only with a very dramatic change in environment. Less marked changes can produce detectable effects, but on the whole studies that look at examination performance in the original lecture room versus the novel examination hall do not suggest any major difference in performance.

The comparatively small effect of environmental context under normal conditions probably reflects the fact that when we are learning, the surroundings are probably not a particularly salient feature of the situation. The internal environment, however, can have subtle but powerful effects. Mood, for instance, can have a contextual effect on memory, with subjects in a sad mood typically being much more likely to recollect earlier unhappy events from their life than subjects in a happy mood, and vice versa.[23] This can have a powerful effect on depression since it will of course tend to make the sad person even sadder, which in turn will cause him or her to remember even more depressing events, locking the unfortunate person into a vicious spiral of increasingly depressive rumination. This is in fact thought to be an important factor in the maintenance of depression, and some relatively recent developments in the cognitive treatment of depression are principally concerned to reverse this process.

Other changes in internal states can of course be induced by drugs, producing so-called *state dependency* effects. Such effects can be produced by alcohol, for example; what is learnt drunk is best recalled drunk. Sometimes alcoholics will hide money or drink while in a drunken state, and then forget where it has been hidden, only to remember once they are drunk again. Such drug-based state dependency did of course play an important role in what is claimed to be the first detective story written, *The Moonstone* of Wilkie Collins.

Retrieval, then, is probably one of the most vulnerable points in human memory, with biased situations leading to failure to recall, or possibly to partial recall, which in turn is subject to distortion when we try to interpret our incomplete memory. A very nice example of such distortion is given by the Swiss psychologist Jean Piaget, who reports having had a very clear and detailed memory of an incident when he was a baby, whereby an attempt was made to kidnap him and was thwarted by his nursemaid. He reports having a very clear and vivid memory of the incident, full of detail. The nursemaid was rewarded for her valour by being given a watch. Many years later she returned the watch to the family saying that she had recently had a religious conversion, and wished to confess an earlier sin. It appears that the incident had simply not occurred, but had been invented by her in the hopes of currying favour with her employers. Piaget's vivid 'memory', it appears, was constructed from the many accounts he had heard of the incident as he grew up.[24]

Before concluding, I should say something about one approach to forgetting that has had considerable influence on twentieth-century western culture, namely the psychoanalytic view of forgetting as the result of repression. Freud suggests that much forgetting occurs because the events concerned are associated with unpleasant events that evoke anxiety, and call up an automatic process that bars them from conscious awareness. In his 'Psychopathology of everyday life',[25] Freud reports many incidents which he attributes to repression. I am afraid, however, that attempts to demonstrate repression under more controlled conditions have not proved particularly encouraging.[26] There certainly is a general tendency for people recalling their earlier life to remember the pleasant events rather than the unpleasant, at least when they are in a reasonably happy state of mind. Whether this represents active repression however is open to question; it is quite possible that this simply reflects a tendency to choose to reflect on and tell others about our successes rather than our failures, leading to pleasant events being rehearsed more. Certainly, attempts to demonstrate the influence of repression under more rigidly controlled conditions tend to suggest that it is not a major feature in the vast amount of forgetting that most people exhibit, although, in the rare cases of hysterical amnesia, something much more closely approaching the Freudian explanation probably does apply.

To conclude, then, I think there is no doubt that human memory is eminently fallible. However, its sources of fallibility are often reflections of its strengths. Bias in feeding information into the memory system certainly does occur, but bias is simply the consequence of selection; if we did not select what was interesting and important, then our memory systems would become overloaded with trivial and irrelevant information.

There is no doubt that forgetting occurs on a massive scale, something that characterizes memory systems in humans but not in computers or libraries. However, such forgetting is on the whole benign. Typically we remember what is salient and important to us, and forget the trivial and irrelevant detail. It is only when such detail subsequently becomes crucial, as in the testimony of an eyewitness, that the fallibility of our memory becomes particularly obvious. In other situations, if we need to remember something in enormous detail, then we write it down.

Finally, retrieval presents a clear bottleneck in our capacity to access what we have previously learnt. Even here, however, the context-dependency effect means that we are more likely to remember the information that is relevant to the situation we are in, in preference to information that is relevant to some other distant setting, surely a sensible adaptation of a limited retrieval system. In conclusion, I would like to suggest that although eminently fallible, human memory is an elegant system; nobody should be without one.

Notes

1   A. D. Baddeley, *Your Memory: A User's Guide*, London: Sidgwick and Jackson, 1982; Penguin, 1983.
2   A. Parkin, *Memory and Amnesia*, Oxford: Blackwell, 1987.

3 R. L. Gregory (ed.), *Oxford Companion to the Mind*, Oxford: Oxford University Press, 1987.

4 G. Hatano and K. Osawa, 'Digit memory of grand experts in abacus-derived mental calculation', *Cognition*, 15 (1983), pp. 95–110.

5 T. Shallice and E. K. Warrington, 'Independent functioning of verbal memory stores: a neuropsychological study', *Quarterly Journal of Experimental Psychology*, 22 (1970), pp. 261–73.

6 A. D. Baddeley, G. Vallar and B. Wilson, 'Sentence comprehension and phonological memory: some neuropsychological evidence', in M. Coltheart (ed.), *Attention and Performance*, vol. 12: *The Psychology of Reading*, London: Lawrence Erlbaum Associates, 1987, pp. 509–29.

7 A. D. Baddeley, C. Papagno and G. Vallar, 'When long-term learning depends on short-term storage', *Journal of Memory and Language*, 27 (1988), pp. 586–95.

8 S. E. Gathercole and A. D. Baddeley (in press), 'Development of vocabulary in children depends on short-term phonological memory', *Journal of Memory and Language*.

9 A. F. Jorm, 'Specific reading retardation and working memory: A review', *British Journal of Psychology*, 74 (1983), pp. 311–42.

10 N. Ellis and B. Large (in press), 'The early states of reading: a longitudinal study', *Applied Cognitive Psychology*.

11 A. D. Baddeley, *Working Memory*, London: Oxford University Press, 1986.

12 E. Tulving, 'Episodic and semantic memory', in E. Tulving and W. Donaldson (eds), *Organization of Memory*, New York: Academic Press, 1972, pp. 381–403.

13 A. J. Wilkins and A. D. Baddeley, 'Remembering to recall in everyday life: an approach to absentmindedness', in M. M. Gruneberg, P. E. Morris and R. N. Sykes (eds), *Practical Aspects of Memory*, London: Academic Press, 1978.

14 M. Moscovitch, 'A neuropsychological approach to memory and perception', in F. I. M. Craik and S. Trehub (eds), *Aging and Cognitive Processes*, New York: Plenum Press, 1982.

15 B. A. Wilson, A. D. Baddeley and J. Cockburn, 'Trials, tribulations and triumphs in the development of a test of everyday memory', in M. M. Gruneberg, P. Morris and P. Sykes (eds), *Practical Aspects of Memory: Current Research and Issues*, vol. 1: *Memory in Everyday Life*, Chichester: John Wiley, 1988, pp. 249–54.

16 Ibid.

17 J. Cockburn and P. T. Smith, in M. M. Gruneberg, P. Morris and P. Sykes (eds), *Practical Aspects of Memory: Current Research and Issues*, vol. 1: *Memory in Everyday Life*, Chichester: John Wiley, 1988.

18 F. Galton, *Inquiries in Human Faculty and its Development*, London: Dent, 1883.
19 A. A. Hastorf and H. Cantrill, 'They saw a game: a case study', *Journal of Abnormal and Social Psychology*, 97 (1954), pp. 339–401.
20 U. Neisser, 'John Dean's memory: a case study', *Cognition*, 9 (1981), pp. 1–22.
21 E. F. Loftus and J. C. Palmer, 'Reconstruction of automobile destruction: an example of the interaction between language and memory', *Journal of Verbal Learning and Verbal Behavior*, 13 (1974), pp. 585–9.
22 D. A. Bekerian and J. M. Bowers, 'Eyewitness testimony: were we misled?', *Journal of Experimental Psychology: Human Learning and Memory*, 9 (1983), pp. 139–45.
23 G. H. Bower, 'Mood and memory', *American Psychologist*, 36 (1981), pp. 129–48.
24 E. F. Loftus, *Eyewitness Testimony*, Cambridge, Mass.: Harvard University Press, 1979, pp. 62–3.
25 S. Freud, 'Psychopathology of everyday life', *The Writings of Sigmund Freud*, ed. A. A. Brill, New York: Modern Library, 1938.
26 A. D. Baddeley, *Your Memory: A User's Guide*, ibid.

3

Memory in Service of Psyche: The Collective Unconscious in Myth, Dream and Ritual

Bani Shorter

It is only too easy to present the subject of memory as if it were a function of the mind alone and to ignore the surprising and erratic emergence of memories which characterize confrontation with the collective unconscious. Yet it is precisely these memories that confound, order and disorder imaginative and psychological life. For psychological life, the conscious awareness of one's identity in relation to one's body and one's meaning, depends upon remembrance of changing images, some of which emerge from pre-existing forms while others are called to mind by personal encounters. Such memories seem less to be compiled than impressed, and when brought to consciousness, which involves selection, choice and evaluation, the picture of a unique person emerges. The process of remembering, classification and integration goes on lifelong in one who is psychologically aware. It expresses the emergence of individuality, individuation and personhood.

In the midst of the conformity characteristic of our modern tribalism, to live as oneself not only takes a strong determination it also requires companionship with those images which dominate our lives. This means stepping aside and taking time off to discover what it is like to be human and ourselves, but most frequently this is not a matter of choice; the necessity is thrust upon us by crisis, breakdown, accident or the ageing process, whether of ourselves or our environment. Yet, when this happens, we inevitably turn to myth, dream and ritual as sources of imaginative renewal, for hope is engendered by the ability to imagine an end that is other than the one that then appears to be inevitable.

Because psychoanalysis involves working with people in crisis, it must give attention both to *how* a person remembers as well as to *what* he or she remembers. For in every personal crisis there is dismemberment of a personal world which previously existed psychologically. Analysis is the painstaking and difficult task of remembering, the slow and arduous reconstellation of a life pattern that is acknowledged, truthful, tolerable, meaningful and individual. It begins, however, with a case history, an anamnesis or recall of a condition which is felt to be *dis*honest, *in*tolerable, meaning*less* and *self-denying*.

Jung's theory of the collective unconscious

During the process of recalling to a person who he or she is, the recapture of hidden memory is crucial. In the early days of psychoanalysis it was assumed that all hidden memories were personally repressed, but very soon it became apparent, to Freud initially, that repressed images such as those encountered in dreams had mythic parallels and disguised ritual sequences. It was Jung who carried these insights further to formulate the existence of the collective unconscious and he was led to do this by way of an image in one of his own dreams.

It was 1909, during the time of his closest collaboration with Freud. The dream which was seminal in Jung's recognition of the collective unconscious was as follows:

> I was in a house I did not know, which had two storeys. It was 'my house.' I found myself in the upper storey, where there was a kind of salon furnished with fine old pieces in rococo style. On the walls hung a number of precious old paintings. I wondered that this should be my house, and thought, 'Not bad.' But then it occurred to me that I did not know what the ground floor looked like. Descending the stairs, I reached the ground floor. There everything was much older, and I realised that this part of the house must date from about the fifteenth and sixteenth century. The furnishings were medieval; the floors were of red brick. Everywhere it was rather dark. I went from one room to another, thinking, 'Now I really must explore the whole house.' I came upon a heavy door, and opened it. Beyond it I discovered a stone

stairway that led down into the cellar. Descending again, I found myself in a beautifully vaulted room which looked exceedingly ancient. Examining the walls, I discovered layers of brick among the ordinary stone blocks, and chips of brick in the mortar. As soon as I saw this I knew that the walls dated from Roman times. My interest by now was intense. I looked more closely at the floor. It was of stone slabs, and in one of these I discovered a ring. When I pulled it, the stone slab lifted, and again I saw a stairway of narrow stone steps leading down into the depths. These, too, I descended, and entered a low cave cut into the rock. Thick dust lay on the floor, and in the dust were scattered bones and broken pottery, like remains of a primitive culture. I discovered two human skulls, obviously very old and half disintegrated.[1]

'Certain questions had been much on my mind during the days preceding [my] dream', Jung writes. They were: 'What is the relation of the almost exclusive personalism of psychoanalysis to general historical assumptions? My dream was giving me the answer. It obviously pointed to the foundations of cultural history – a history of successive layers of consciousness. My dream thus constituted a kind of structural diagram of the human psyche; it postulated something of an altogether *impersonal* nature underlying that psyche.'[2]

What the dreamer saw 'was that the house represented an image of the psyche . . . that is to say, of [the dreamer's] state of consciousness with hitherto unconscious additions.' In spite of its somewhat outmoded style, the salon looked as if it were inhabited and, to Jung, it suggested the 'first level of consciousness' where he resided. But the deeper he went, he reported, 'the more alien and darker the scene became'. 'In the cave', he writes, 'I discovered remains of . . . the world of primitive man within myself – a world which can scarcely be reached or illuminated by consciousness. . . . It was my first inkling', he says, 'of a collective apriori beneath the personal psyche.'[3]

Thus Jung was launched on a lifelong quest for answers as to how the 'collective apriori' serves psyche, the place and purpose of a collective unconscious in psychological ecology. If the capacity for imaginative regeneration from a pre-existing source is a reservoir of psychic health, then it becomes urgent that we make use of it, asking ourselves (as Jung immediately did, to the severance of his dependence upon Freud, his mentor and guide) whether the models we bring to bear upon interpretation of personal psychic contents are adequate, accurate, sufficiently profound and differentiated. Moreover, do they embrace enough of what we understand it means to be human? For it is insufficient to assume a perspective which is purely and exclusively personal. This does not enable us to encompass the circumference of psyche's involvement, which appears at one and the same time to be concerned both with the microcosm and the macrocosm. Jung had been brought up against these issues in an abrupt and abiding form, through intervention of the dream, and they underlay the questions he addressed to his researches on the nature of dream, myth and ritual from then onwards. He felt himself to be propelled toward nothing less than a study of psychological dynamics in which collective memory was all important.

It is not surprising that Jung's work has been revolutionary for, after 1909, fairly quickly he moved away from emphasis upon treatment of symptoms to the analysis of symbols. 'We have reason to suppose', he wrote not long after his dream, 'that the unconscious is never quiescent in the sense of being inactive, but it is ceaselessly engaged in grouping and regrouping its contents (in relation to consciousness).'[4] And he hypothesized that such grouping and regrouping took place in relation to pre-existing and collective images called archetypes. His subsequent observations of archetypal processes at work in the psyche of modern man led to the conclusion that when we confront psychological distress we must treat nothing less than the whole person. 'Psyche is image; image is psyche', he concluded.[5] But an image can not be defined or reproduced; it can only be described. Thus treatment involving the recall and description of imagery became the foundation of a method of psychotherapy hitherto unpractised in modern times.

Dreams and healing

There is a connection between Jung's observations and hypotheses and the crises which are brought to present-day consulting

rooms. Persons approach psychoanalysts and other psycho-
therapists bringing their broken, malformed and misguided
images of man, woman and God. Such images are no longer
collectively maintained in forms which are adequate to the crises
people feel and, so, they turn to the spontaneous resources of
their own psyches (the collective unconscious) – their dreams,
the replay of myth and sources of innate ritual within themselves
– for restoration of likenesses which they can trust. They do so
by analysis of unspecified symbols, with the help of others who
are prepared to investigate such imagery from both a personal
and a collective point of view.

Fairly recently two dreams have been brought to me which are
illustrative of the collective apriori about which Jung spoke and
to some extent these dreams are also analogous to his dream of
1909. Neither was dreamed by someone who had made a
detailed study of Jung's work, however. Yet both of the
dreamers were persons who faced difficult crises in mid-life and
were forced to consider rending changes. Neither felt that there
were personal resources sufficient to cope with what was
demanded.

The first of the dreams was dreamed by a woman and was as
follows:

> I was setting out for therapy. I had a relatively short distance to
> travel but there was a question of the route to be taken. I was told
> that I could not use the road that existed but neither could I take
> the lane that had been there before the road was built. I would
> lose my way on the path that once wound among the trees. To
> reach my therapist I would have to travel by way of the trace
> which lay under the earth before a path, a lane or street was
> evident.

The second was dreamed by a man:

> A well-known company operates a big hotel in the north. I arrive
> at the site and recognize the building as one of the grandest of its
> kind. It is built on land reclaimed from a marsh.
>
> I then see the marsh as it was before the building was
> constructed. Great stone blocks had been put in place to form a

foundation. They will not sink. They have been there for a very long time and were originally laid down for the building of a fortification.

Now I am present as the foundation stones for this ancient earthwork are laid. I am one of the workmen. The outline of the master plan is in my mind and I am digging a long trench to receive the first stones.

Such dreams suggest that 'the grip of the study of history on the face of culture can be a mere fingerhold.'[6] In the phenomenology of a case history, there is already something very old. Such remnants would be of interest only to the biographer or archivist were they not also of immediate relevance to the individual, bringing him into touch with his contemporary ancestors, as it were, and facilitating recovery. For in every personal crisis not only is there dismemberment of a world as it has previously existed for a person psychologically, but known and conscious resources are depleted or no longer available. Consequently, there has been a breakdown of confidence. Psychoanalysts are asked to assist in helping to reassemble lives which are felt to be falling apart and in such situations the reminder that the foundations of the structure were laid down long ago or the awareness that the street follows a memory trace of an inherent path can be reassuring.

The more so because such images appear to arise from a source beyond conscious control. But not all such imagery is benign. There is often little resemblance between so-called logical, traceable and rational memories and the emotion-laden pictures which inhabit the unconscious psyche. For the memory of the collective unconscious does not appear to be selective; it is merely the heritage of the species, coloured, distorted and weighted very little by historical trends or cultural context. The archetypal images with which our lives are impressed, the primal possibilities of human expression, are both dark and light. It is in relation to them that a person is tested, and the infinite possibilities of building on that foundation allow the person freedom to express individuality. Pathology becomes manifest when the eternal images themselves take control.

Mythology and the archetypes

During the decades which followed his dream Jung lent himself as a researcher to the investigation of evidence of the collective unconscious at work in the psyche of man and, as a doctor, to its usefulness in healing modern illness and afflictions. He began with observations of the behaviour of his own psyche as the empirical material to which he had most immediate and intimate access; he also had daily opportunities to observe the psychic workings of patients in his psychiatric and analytic practices. He deplored the over-emphasis upon rationality evident at that time and he saw the rediscovery of the unconscious as compensatory to trends which seemed destined to annihilate our conscious world, a conclusion based upon the final evidence of two world wars. He was convinced that, left to ourselves, we would destroy life by obsessive and one-sided dependence upon consciousness.

He concluded that the healing potential of the collective unconscious lay in two factors; in its compensatory or balancing function and in the energizing effect of its imagery. The force of the archetype is such as to demand expression, a power strong enough to effect a take-over or possession of the individual psyche if there is not a compensatory image available to consciousness. What happens then becomes a replay of a mythic rather than a personal theme. But in the so-called normal person dream symbolism compensates this drastic and collective tendency. Choice becomes available; one is not swept away by the tremendous and compelling counter-energies latent in primordial and unconscious imagery. In daily life the dream operates in such a way as to counter-balance or offset extreme dependence on either one or the other pull of archetypal possibility, whether positive or negative. Through the impact and message of the dream we are caused to remember ourselves, as it were.

The capacity to expose ever-recurring and energizing images effectively communicated as personal symbols thus appears as one function of the collective unconscious. But as an activating and energizing, stimulating and animating existential force, the collective unconscious also shapes our lives by insisting upon

encounter with root metaphors. Through the dream it engages
us with a fundamental imagery coexistent among our fellow
human beings and coeternal with the experience of man, yet
personalized by exposure to our own circumstances. Whether or
not the exposure is purposive, and how it may be purposive in a
god-intended sense, is a separate though related question. For left
to itself, deprived of man's conscious interrelationship and interaction, there will be only a replay of mythic themes, an acting
out of recurring subplots rather than an enactment of a life's
story unfolding as a person's own.

In the *Myth of the Eternal Return*, Eliade, a contemporary,
friend and collaborator of Jung, writes of mythology that it
provides a matrix of 'ontological conception' since 'an object or
an act becomes real only in so far as it imitates or repeats an
archetype . . .; everything which lacks an exemplary model is
meaningless.'[7] The mythical epoch is the time when the archetypes
were first revealed. Remembering them, we project ourselves
back into that time, and any repetition of an archetypal gesture
affirms being in a profoundly elemental sense. At that time and
in that place man remembers himself and his reality is confirmed.

For the psychologist the network of world mythologies
provides a contour map of 'the inscape of the soul'. It shows the
crevasses and the passes, the lanes and paths (i.e. the footpath and
the ancient foundations of our dreamers), the cliffs and shoals,
the heights of inflation and the depths of despair, the summits
and valleys, the sources of water for the traveller and the
occasional settlement for rest. In myth we have mapped out,
localized and made imaginatively intelligible every device by
which the 'eternal' has intervened in the life of man to date. Jung
recognized it as the supreme interlocking model of the
remembered imagery of humanity, a model to which one is
unconsciously turned and returned by the necessity to explain
and heal oneself. No longer is the science of mythology to be
seen as a misguided attempt to explain the workings of gods
believed in by less enlightened peoples. 'The gods', viewed
psychologically, are the omnipresent archetypal metaphors, and
in their workings man sees reflected that which is at work within
himself.

'Dream is the personalized myth, myth the depersonalized dream; both myth and dream are symbolic in the same general way of the dynamics of the psyche. But in the dream the forms are quirked by the peculiar troubles of the dreamer, whereas in myth the problems and solutions shown are directly valid for all mankind.'[8]

Since myths deal with archetypal truths, no one 'lives out' a myth; those few who feel they know their myths have sensed a relevance between their life's characteristics and those of a mythic figure. One is reminded of Perseus, a hero half mortal, half immortal, setting out to slay Medusa by cutting off her head, the sight of which turned humans to stone. To do so he had to travel to the far edge of the habitable world, to the realm of night. And who could have lent him the winged shoes but Hermes, the bringer of dreams?[9] But Athene lent him a shield to be used at the time of confrontation, one highly polished, in which the reflected image of the Gorgon could be held, so that, approaching her, he would not be subjected to the fate of fixation.[10] Myths are used as polished reflectors against the inhumanity of lives fixated either in consciousness or in unconsciousness.

At a time of dismemberment and personal crisis, in the psychological fragments of a split world, we find mythic elements. In this regard, the dream of a woman in her early fifties is dramatically illustrative. She was a person perennially traumatized by events of her early childhood which had been such as to cause her to return there in memory and fear ever afterward. Her dream was as follows:

Once again I was back in the place where I was born and lived as a child. I was walking through the city and entered a park which had become a sculpture garden. I was attracted by the many statues which appeared to have been sculpted in the style of my youth. As I strolled about among them I became aware of a strange feeling that they wanted to communicate something to me. There was something I could do for them; they wanted me to feed them. There, surrounded by shrubbery, I came upon a statue of myself aged nine. As I stood looking at it, it reached out its

arms of stone and with a soundless voice begged me for
nourishment.

Here myth and dream reflect one another, as in a gleaming
shield. As always, myth reaffirms being by an imaginative
statement of our inevitabilities. The weight of centuries of
recurrent enactment, belief and retelling has pressed these stories
deep into our lives and personalities. They are part of a collective
memory which intercedes between us and god-like forces. They
are at the interface of being and becoming, and interpretation
involves a long, deep remembering so that it is possible to glean
from such mythologems as were provided for this woman a
sense of continuity and validation. For myth is perennial, while
most biographies are effaced with the passage of time.

Ritual and healing

In the autumn of 1977, several years after dreaming her dream,
the dreamer sent me from America a short poem which had
appeared in the *New Yorker*, entitled 'The statues'. It begins:
'Who shall feed the statues?' and continues: 'Through what
mouths do they receive the nourishment of our gaze?'

Finding the poem rekindled the dreamer's memory of a
perennial continuity which was ritually contained in the analytic
hours we had spent together. Here it is proper to speak of ritual,
for work at the interface of archetypal and personal realities
demands the containment and assurance that only ritual provides.
For all ritual is consecrated in the sense that it is presided over by
a god-image, whether consciously apprehended or not by the
participants, a presence which with objectivity *orders* the rite.
And it is in this sense that Jung speaks of the collective
unconscious as 'the objective psyche'.

'Rituals reveal values at their deepest level . . . men (and
women) express in ritual what moves them most.'[11] At the same
time: 'Ritual is the natural, necessary and transitional carrier of
psychological process.'[12] As a therapist/observer of individual
change, time and again I have been surprised by the spontaneous
enactment of ritual, even when the person involved had no
conscious knowledge of the meaning or universality of the rite

employed. When the time is right, it is as if psyche then remembers what the conscious mind has been trained to forget and the person is impelled to enact a ritual sequence.

Part of *An Image Darkly Forming: Women and Initiation* is devoted to a description of the spontaneous rituals enacted during analytic therapy. There I speak of Jen, an untutored woman with few means, who had lived her life in the guise of a young boy. After an extended and painful period of recalling to herself that she was feminine, an analysis lasting two and a half years, and when she was nearly fifty years of age, she could at last refer to the feminine within herself as 'she' and she spontaneously enacted a rite of adolescent initiation, reporting to me:

> 'I want to tell you that I took her into the city and gave her a Christmas present' . . .
> 'What did you give her?' I enquired.
> There was a pause. 'It took courage and all my money but I put holes in her ears and I bought her gold rings to wear so she'd remember she's a woman for ever and ever', Jen said.

When the moment for initiation comes there is an instinctive feel for what is needed. This and other devised rituals which I have witnessed have broken forth as if in eruption from the reservoir of archaic symbols, promptings and metaphors that Jung held to be the collective memory of all of us and which he named the collective unconscious. As with the dream, the force of the thrust and the symbolism employed proportionally compensate the consciousness of the individual. But the balance of remembering is not merely a technical feat or balancing act. What is registered by the individual is an increase in consciousness of what it means to be human and the one he or she is. It is an ontological balancing, symbolically expressed.

From dis-membering to re-membering

It is for the frightening, often overwhelming transitional movement from one state of being to the incarnation of another that rituals are devised and employed. Dis-membering is marked by disintegration of a previous state, while re-membering, psychologically speaking, pertains to the assemblage of a more complete and authentic person, effected by confrontation with eternal verities of superior power and purpose. For the blow that shatters a person is always stronger than the ego, alluded to as 'bigger than I am'. Consequently, re-membering is completed by consciousness of the image and purpose of whatever I then know to be 'bigger than I am'.

The dismemberment of a personal crisis seems designed to pin-point relations with invisible and superior forces. However ugly, belittling, estranging, dark and devil-ridden it may be registered in the first place as being, it can also be seen as a summons to the discovery of who we are and from a psychological perspective it points to an enhancement rather than a diminishment of what we were. Hence, it can be viewed as compensatory to a former condition rather than merely as a judgement.

Yet I suppose the association which first springs to mind for most of us in regard to dis-memberment has to do with torture and martyrdom. It was a punishment for wrong-doing or used in retaliation for wrong-conviction, so the memory of judgement lingers. When depicted in medieval illustrations, however, we often see the severed head set apart as if to watch the process so that, we may infer, the observing eye of the soul, the logos of being, shall see and not forget. It was left to early Christians to interpret this as separation from the body in preparation for a life of the spirit, when they would be remembered and at one with their God. The analogy with the life of their Saviour is obvious.

At the same time, the myth of renewal by dismemberment has been handed down in folklore from quite different sources as well; from ancient Greece, India, central Asia and Siberia. It is a common and recurring motif in the ritual initiation of Shamanic healers. The sickness of the Shaman, which justifies or denies his vocation, is symbolized by dismemberment and it becomes a validation of his powers if he is able to translate the experience into healing knowledge to be used for himself and others. In the space which intervenes between his dismemberment and remembering, he is exposed to the possibility of learning the language of the intent of dismemberment by spirit and from the personal soul.

Again, it is of interest that when dismemberment takes place and the head is severed in vision, it is set aside 'for the candidate must watch [this] with his own eyes. Later, when waking from the experience, as from a deep sleep, the initiate remembers himself as who he is, renewed.'[13] The eyes symbolize consciousness, awareness, seeing and experiencing the dismemberment of crisis in an ontological light which is analogous to the perception of one's purpose or vocation as an individual.

The urgings of dream, myth and ritual overpower and dismember our reason. All three are symbolic and metaphoric expressions of possibilities as well. Yet, however much a person may choose to ignore, repress or otherwise avoid the power of unconscious promptings, they do not diminish. On the contrary, they increase. The dream repeats; it becomes the nightmare. Too late, perhaps, we discover that myth is being played out and it is real. A need for ritual asserts itself forcibly at life's imminent crises – birth, adolescence, mid-life, preparation for death and death itself. Our psychic imagery, the picture language of our souls, demands and provides a middle ground, spoken of as a *mesocosm* by Joseph Campbell, where we struggle with the limits of our humanity on the borders of ultimate mystery. For the encounters require time and space for the projections of an unconscious god-image to be faced. There, within the matrix of the mesocosm and by way of symbolic exchange, we transact our destinies and recollect our souls.

In his final work, Gregory Bateson spoke of the double bind of our time as being between 'rigour' and 'imagination' and made the bold statement that 'rigour alone is paralytic death but imagination alone is insanity.'[14] Rigour and imagination provide two ways of perceiving which the collective unconscious naturally unites and fuses by way of psychological metaphor. When Jung spoke of a 'supra-ordinate principle' governing psyche or referred to it as a god-image, he called both the principle and the image the *self* but he avoided naming its source. Had he done so, he would have far exceeded his brief as a psychiatrist and analyst. But the omission (and we do not know whether Jung avoided naming the name of the patterner for himself) illustrates and calls our attention to the culminating function of pattern inherent in the collective unconscious. It is by way of crisis that both person and psyche are recalled to their natures and to their gods. The dismembering of life patterns causes us to forget names no longer relevant for things named. And, at that time, inevitably we are without memory for the name of what is re-membering us. We are freed then from conceptualizations so that the characteristics of a transforming image can be received and recognized as part of our being. But *being*, remembered, remembers a name for that which recalls it. That is to say, the process of remembering that I exist, and how I exist as I, includes verification; but whether or not that is Verity neither Jung nor I is enabled to say.

Notes

1 C. G. Jung, *Memories, Dreams, Reflections*, ed. A. Jaffé, tr. R. and C. Winston, London: Collins, 1963, p. 155.
2 Ibid., p. 161.
3 Ibid., pp. 160 ff.
4 C. G. Jung, *The Collected Works*, vol. 7, tr. R. F. C. Hull, London: Routledge & Kegan Paul, 1966, para. 204.
5 Ibid., vol. 13, 1973, para. 75.
6 P. Brown, *Society and the Holy in Late Antiquity*, London: Faber and Faber, 1982, p. 4.
7 M. Eliade, *The Myth of the Eternal Return: or, Cosmos and History*, tr. Willard R. Trask, Princeton: Princeton University Press, 1974, p. 34.
8 J. Campbell, *Hero with a Thousand Faces*, New York: World Publishing Company, 1970, p. 19.
9 C. Kerényi, *The Heroes of the Greeks*, tr. H. J. Rose, London: Thames and Hudson, 1974, p. 49.
10 N. Micklem, 'The intolerable image: the mythic background of psychosis', *Spring*, 1979, pp. 1 ff.
11 M. Wilson, 'Nikymyakyusa ritual in symbolism', *American Anthropological Review*, 36 (2) (1954), p. 231. Quoted in V. Turner, *The Ritual Process: Structure and Anti-structure*, Ithaca: Cornell University Press, 1979, p. 6. See also C. G. Jung, *Collected Works*, vol. 18, para. 617.

12 B. Shorter, *An Image Darkly Forming: Women and Initiation*, London: Routledge & Kegan Paul, 1987, p. 43.

13 M.Eliade, *Shamanism, Archaic Techniques of Ecstasy*, tr. Willard R. Trask, Princeton: Princeton University Press, 1974, p. 36.

14 G. Bateson, *Mind and Nature: A Necessary Unity*, New York: Bantam Books, 1980, p. 242.

4

Memory and Oral Tradition
Krinka Vidaković Petrov

One of the oldest and most widespread metaphors in our culture is the one which identifies the world with a book. Christians thought that God's greatest creation was the Book of the Universe. The Jewish mystics proposed that the instruments of his creation were numbers and letters. Followers of the Greek philosopher Plato conceived of the stars as eternal letters written in the heavens, while the great astronomer Galileo Galilei spoke of the Book of the Universe written in a mathematical language consisting of triangles and circles. Mystics, philosophers and scientists alike have defined the world as a cosmos opposed to chaos, as a Book written with various kinds of signs – letters, numbers, triangles. The Book, therefore, stands as a model of the world, a model created with signs of one or another order.

This basic idea has reached our own century in the form of information theory and semiotics. Culture itself is defined as a book consisting of manifold texts. A text may be any message communicated through a system of signs and organized according to a certain code. Culture, therefore, consists of signs, codes and messages whereby we create a model of the world, translating – so to say – the open world of reality into the closed world of the text.

The word 'text' is used in a broad sense. Usually we associate it with natural languages, and the linguistic symbols or visual signs (alphabets) in which they are recorded. But texts imply other sign systems as well: by 'text' we may mean a painting, a ballet performance, a film. Any sign system we use, however, must rely on memory. Culture itself is memory, indicating the power of the system to preserve and accumulate information. Culture is memory – created, preserved, accumulated and transmitted by human society.[1]

When we say memory, another word immediately comes to mind: oblivion. Memory implies both remembering and forgetting; it implies a choice, a discrimination between items which will be preserved and those which will be suppressed. As a mechanism inherent to memory, oblivion is creative. But as an instrument susceptible to manipulation from the outside, it can be destructive. In medieval times, men considered to be heretics were burned at the stake. And so were books. In our own times the Nazis used fire for the extermination of people. And fire was used to destroy the memory of their culture embodied in books. When my home town – Belgrade – was bombed in 1941, one of the main targets was the National Library. It contained only books and manuscripts. But these were the written records of a culture which had to share the fate of its protagonists – the people.

Techniques of oral transmission

Apart from the library of written records, there is another 'library' – that of the oral tradition. Illiterate societies as well as those in which literacy is confined to small circles have, nonetheless, developed rich cultures which have been preserved in and transmitted by the oral tradition.

A well-known and extremely interesting example, involving both oral and written communication, is the Bible, which marks the beginning of the cult of writing in our culture. When we read the New Testament we are aware that the Gospel appears in four versions, stemming ultimately from oral sources, although in the form in which they came down to us there is reason to suppose the influence of written as well as oral texts (some Biblical scholars, for example, believe that Mark may well have preceded and influenced Luke and Matthew).[2] Such intermediate written influence notwithstanding, the existence of these four versions points to the types of shifts occurring in oral communication, namely, that a story or song has a latent existence in the memory of a performer and is actualized only when orally performed and communicated. Every performance, however, may produce a new variant or version, since it is unlikely that the text would be reproduced exactly. First, because human memory is imperfect (the performer could simply forget the exact wording of a line or sentence). Secondly, the singer in the oral tradition is not bound by an objectively existing original (any version may be as 'original' as any other). Thirdly, the performer may deliberately choose to adjust his or her performance to the expectations of the audience, in order to get a favourable response.

We can imagine a singer, for example, who tends to memorize the literal wording of a song in order to carry out a fairly accurate reproduction. The singer is somewhat like a person learning a foreign language, learning by heart every sentence in order to repeat it exactly. But anyone who has tried learning a foreign language knows that the only way to accomplish this is by studying not only the words and the forms, but also the grammar, which shows us how to construct meaningful sentences. The singer is in a similar position. He or she must know the 'grammar' of the tradition. For example, a singer asked to perform a funeral song is not free to do whatever she pleases. On the contrary, she must know the details of the funeral ceremony, the meaning and function of each segment and the moment she is expected to sing; she must know what she is to sing about and how this is to be done. Memory, therefore, can be passive, implying the preservation of a given message in order to have it reproduced fairly accurately. Active memory, on the other hand, is creative; it involves the utilization of the 'grammar' one must know in order to produce and change messages, thus allowing the singer to 'speak the language' of the tradition.

Every time the singer performs, he or she is resorting to two devices: repetition and variation. When we have heard several performances of a song or tale, we can distinguish between features repeated in a succession of versions, as well as traits specific to each individual text. Both repetition and variation can be carried out at various levels of the text.

Among the most prominent repetitive elements are formulas:

groups of words used regularly to express the same meaning under the same metrical conditions. The formula is constant in its meaning, its wording and its metrical value.[3]

Another technique used by singers in the oral tradition is paraphrase: rendering the meaning in a different form. Paraphrase implies repetition of meaning, but variation of wording through changes in word order, shifts in sentence structure, substitution of synonyms, etc. It is not restricted to oral texts, but is found in all texts – written or oral – that exist in several versions or variants. The following example from the Gospels is quoted only because it is so familiar:

> . . . that this night, before the cock crow, thou shalt deny me thrice . . .

> . . . that this day, even in this night, before the cock crow twice, thou shalt deny me thrice . . .

> . . . the cock shall not crow this day, before that thou shalt thrice deny that thou knowest me . . .

> . . . the cock shall not crow, till thou hast denied me thrice.[4]

Variation can also be effected by preserving the structure of the sentence and substituting certain elements.

Repetition and variation can be shown at higher levels of the text where they involve narrative units such as plots, sequences, scenes, characters and motifs. The plot consists of elements which some folklorists, following the Russian scholar Propp, have called *functions*.[5] In fairy tales, for example, there are functions which have been defined as 'prohibition', 'violation of prohibition', 'triumph of the hero over the antagonist', etc. A prohibition takes the form of an order, but in the actual texts this can be expressed in a number of different ways: in one sentence or a sequence of sentences, as one action or another, using different verbs. Such variations, however, do not change the meaning of this function in the overall structure of the tale. As for scenes and characters, many of these are type scenes and stock characters repeated in one version after another. Furthermore, repetition can be used within the song as well. The same lines may be moved from one dialogue or narrative segment to another, from direct into indirect speech and back again, with very slight changes in verb tense or pronouns. This is a simple but quite useful device, often applied in Serbo-Croatian narrative songs. As a specific type of parallelism, it is also used in lyrical songs. In the famous song on the death of the mother of the Jugović heroes, eight lines are organized according to this kind of repetition. First the narrator describes the mother praying to God that he may give her 'the eyes of a falcon' and 'the white wings of a swan' so that she could fly to the battlefield at Kosovo; then he repeats this by describing how God answered her prayers, how he gave her the eyes of a falcon and the white wings of a swan, and so she flew to Kosovo.

> Boga moli Jugovića majka:
> Da joj Bog da oči sokolove
> I bijela krila labudova,
> Da odleti na Kosovo ravno . . .
> Što molila, Boga domolila:
> Bog joj dao oči sokolove
> I bijela krila labudova,
> Ona leti na Kosovo ravno . . .[6]

Formulaic diction, paraphrase, substitutions, functions, type scenes and stock characters all show that oral transmission is necessarily based on the repetition of certain patterns, as well as on variation. Both the singer and the audience are aware of these patterns. Although they are individuals, first and foremost they are members of the community, sharing the memory common to the community as a whole, memory which is the source of its cultural identity.

Folklore and history

As we have seen, the information preserved in the memory of the community can be varied in nature. A specific kind of information we would like to comment on is the awareness of past events relevant to the life of the community. We have all noticed that some folk songs tend to describe their story as occurring at a definite time and place, claiming that the events they speak of are true. History is considered to be a truthful account of past events, and many folk songs claim to be 'historical' in this sense. However, we must bear in mind that what the song actually contains is usually an interpretation of certain historical data, an interpretation which often tends to combine history (fact) with legend (fiction). Thus, historical truth is adapted to narrative patterns typical of legends.

In the Serbian tradition the central cycle of 'historical' songs deals with a crucial event in Serbian history: the battle of Kosovo which took place in June 1389. The defeat in this battle marks the downfall of the Serbian state and the beginning of Turkish rule over Serbian lands. Kosovo was liberated by the Serbian army only in 1912, during the Balkan Wars. A journalist following the soldiers wrote a report dated 10 October 1912 which reads: 'Mass was held today at Kosovo, and a requiem for Lazar at the place where he was killed . . . the first Christian Orthodox mass at this site after more than five hundred years.'[7] Lazar was the king who led the Serbian army in the battle. Other protagonists of the Kosovo cycle are his wife Milica, the Jugović family, Miloš Obilić – who killed the Turkish sultan Murad – and Vuk Branković. The interpretation of the Kosovo theme is heavily laden with emotion, and attention is focused not on the battle itself, but on events preceding it and consequences following the battle.

In an anonymous account of these events written several decades afterwards, the conflict is interpreted in religious terms. It is described as a battle between the soldiers of Christ and the Ishmaelites (Turks). Lazar is described as saying to his men: 'Our duty is to die. Let us shed our blood so that in death we find redemption.' The dead king is compared to Joshua, who led his people (the dead soldiers) to the 'promised land'. The anonymous writer also says King Lazar was killed and beheaded.[8]

All these elements were later absorbed by the oral tradition. In the song known as 'The downfall of the kingdom of Serbia', Lazar is asked to choose between a heavenly and an earthly crown, between winning the battle with the Turks and perishing in it. This is how the scene is rendered in the song:

'If I choose a kingdom,
Choose a kingdom on earth,
An earthly kingdom is only for a short time,
But the heavenly one is eternal, and for ever.'
The king wanted the heavenly kingdom
Rather than the earthly one,
So he built a church at Kosovo.
He didn't make its foundation of marble,
But of pure silk and scarlet cloth . . .
Then he had the army take communion,
    and gave them their orders.[9]

Another song describes the supper at Lazar's court on the eve of the battle. Lazar doubts the loyalty of Miloš Obilić, who answers him:

I have never been a traitor –
Have never been nor will I ever be,
But tomorrow at Kosovo I intend
To die for the Christian faith;
The traitor sits at your side
Drinking wine at your sleeve.[10]

In still another song we are told how Lazar's head was found by a boy who put it into a spring, where it remained for forty years until it was discovered by a teamster. He plunges into the water and lifts out 'the holy head of Lazar' and places it on the grass. But then a miracle happens:

The head vanished from the green grass,
The head moved by itself across the field,
The holy head joining the holy body,
Just the way it was before.[11]

These examples indicate a tendency to interpret historical facts according to legendary narrative patterns borrowed from the Bible. Three key biblical motifs are included here: the sacrifice necessary for redemption after death, the treason foretold at the Last Supper and the resurrection after death. Thus the oral tradition, preserving its specific modes of expression, absorbs elements from both history and legend. This particular combination was especially functional at the beginning of the nineteenth century, when most of these songs were collected, because this was the time of the two major Serbian uprisings which would lead to the liberation of the nation and the renewal of statehood.

The Kosovo songs show how oral tradition adapts history to legendary patterns. The next example will show the opposite process – how fairy tale patterns can absorb elements from history.

Folklore and archetypal themes

Fairy tales are fictional by definition. Whatever action there is happens 'once upon a time'. A widespread fairy tale motif is 'the husband's return home in time to prevent his wife's re-marriage'.[12] Apart from the *Odyssey* and tales, it is also found in ballads collected throughout Europe. The Scottish versions of *Hind Horn*[13] tell how the princess gives the hero a magic ring; after seven years of absence he returns and is told by a beggar that the princess is about to get married; disguised as a beggar, the hero asks the bride for a drink, then he drops the ring into the cup and thus is recognized and the marriage is prevented. In the Modern Greek versions the hero is a prisoner; on returning home he meets his father pruning the vineyard; he is finally recognized by his wife thanks to the ring. The Serbian version, 'The captivity of Janković Stojan', is based on the same narrative pattern, but the hero is identified as a historic person, the real Stojan Janković from the seventeenth century. He was a famous local hero who participated in many of the battles fought between Venice and Turkey, and as such he is the protagonist of various epic songs (both Christian and Moslem). Research has shown that Stojan Janković was in fact captured by the Turks and taken prisoner to Istanbul, but that he managed to escape and return home after fourteen months.[14] The folk song tells us that Stojan was captured in the war, that he left behind a recently wedded wife, that he spent nine years in prison before he could escape and return; he meets his mother in the vineyard and after a series of events his identity is revealed and the remarriage of his wife prevented. This is an example of how the oral tradition transforms the 'once upon a time' of a fairy tale by determining the time and place of action and identifying the hero with a historical person, adapting the narrative pattern to the requirements of another genre – the epic song.

The following examples concerning history and legend will show how oral and written literature converge at certain points.

In the tenth and eleventh centuries there was a Slavic kingdom called Duklja (Doclea) located in the region between Montenegro, Dalmatia and Albania. It was ruled early in the eleventh century by a king called Vladimir. According to a Byzantine chronicle, he was married to a cousin of Samuel, the king of Bulgaria. Vladimir was a righteous ruler, but finally he was tricked by Samuel's successors and killed.[15] A later chronicle contains a legendary version of Vladimir's life, combining elements of hagiography and romance; it relates how Vladimir was taken prisoner by the Bulgarian king, later released and then married to his daughter Kosara, who became queen of Vladimir's restored kingdom.[16] This story was highlighted by Andrija Kačić-Miošić, an eighteenth-century Franciscan monk, author of the very popular *A Pleasant Discourse About the Slavic People*. This book contains a number of his poems written in imitation of folk songs, one of them being a ballad of King Vladimir and his wife Kosara. The ballad includes a dialogue between the prisoner and the king's daughter, one between the princess and her father, the scene of Vladimir's release and the description of the wedding.[17] Variants of this song and others written by Kačić-Miošić were later collected and published as authentic folk songs from the oral tradition.[18]

Actually, the oral tradition does include a number of real folk songs based on this narrative pattern. In one of them the hero is none other than Marko Kraljević who escapes from an 'Arab' king's dungeon with the help of the king's daughter, whom he promises to marry. (He does not keep his promise.[19]) In other songs the hero is Stojan Janković. In one we are told how Stojan is caught and taken prisoner by Mustay-bey; but his sister Haikuna falls in love with the prisoner, tricks her brother into giving her the keys, flees with Stojan and finally converts to

Christianity, marrying him.[20] Quoting M. Halansky, T. Maretić points out non-Slavic sources containing the same narrative pattern based on the motif of 'the jailor's daughter', including the Byzantine epic poem about Digenes Akritas and the tenth-century German poem about Waltharius.[21]

These examples illustrate how three real persons who lived in different historical periods, Vladimir, Marko Kraljević and Stojan Janković, have been associated with the same motif of 'the jailor's daughter', elaborated in a narrative pattern widespread in both oral tradition and written literary sources. They also show how the oral tradition moves freely through various levels of memory, involving elements of both form and content. The freedom with which this is done emphasizes the power of oral tradition to adjust itself to the roles folklore assumes in the life of the community.

Oral tradition, ritual and time

'Historical' folk songs describe time as a linear process. In folklore, however, there is a large number of lyrical songs which express a cyclical concept of time. Such are the calendar songs associated with the succession of seasons and the periodic regeneration of nature. Another group of songs deals with the cycle of human life – birth, the coming of age, marriage, death. These are the key points in the life of the individual as well as in the family, which is considered to be a very important social unit. They all have to do with kinship relations, which are extremely important in primitive societies and therefore tend to be ritualized. The ritual confirms these events as socially accepted facts and as such they are given a highly symbolical meaning.

Rituals are based on archaic beliefs translated into customs, which tradition preserves as a guarantee of the stability and continuity of the community. The custom itself can even survive the loss of its original meaning. Customs are deeply rooted in tradition and are imposed by the authority of being something transmitted from one generation to the next, something people living today share with their ancestors. This is an extremely important factor of identity for the community and it rests on the fact that its members partake in a common consciousness, one shared with the members of the same community in the past. Unlike other folk songs, ritual songs from the oral tradition contain information on the archaic past – the deepest layer of memory.

Death is a universal experience every individual and community has to cope with and translate into a text containing our emotional, psychological, social and cultural responses. If you were to go today to a Serbian village and visited the cemetery, you might see an astonishing scene: people seated around the grave eating and drinking. This is the *daća*,[22] a ritual feast held at the grave on the fortieth day after the funeral of the deceased. The feast includes two obligatory elements: *koljivo*, which is a kind of cooked wheat, and red wine. The participants of the feast sit around the grave, and it used to be the custom to leave a vacant place for the soul of the dead person, since according to old beliefs he or she was expected to visit the world of the living on this day. This is more or less the way this custom was observed many centuries ago, even before Christianity. A modernized version is practised today in the cities, not because people nowadays believe in communication with the dead, but because it is a custom inherited from the distant past of the community and Christianized by the Orthodox church.

The ritual songs performed at funerals and on certain subsequent occasions are especially interesting from the point of view of memory. What is specific to them is the fact that memory is expanded in order to include both the living and the dead. Why? The cult of the dead implies the coexistence of two worlds: the world of the living and that of the dead. In terms of time this means that the past – associated with one's ancestors – is simultaneous with the present. The ancestors are, therefore, integrated into the present life of the community. Whenever the individual or the community is threatened, the living can evoke their dead ancestors and secure their protection. In order to do this there must be a way of communicating with the dead and reminding them of the living. What is expected of the ancestors is to remember their descendants, to preserve them in their memory.

There are many ways of communicating with the dead, all based on magic. According to old beliefs, there are certain places in the house where one can expect the souls of ancestors to appear. One such place is the corner of a room: this explains the Christmas custom of throwing walnuts into the corners of a room as an offering to the dead.[23] Another place is the attic: this is why it was a custom that during a wedding feast the mother-in-law would go up to the attic and dance there alone, in order to secure the blessings of the ancestors for the bride and groom.[24]

Funeral and wedding laments

Still another way of communicating with the dead is the funeral song. It is always in the form of a monologue addressed to the deceased, who is considered to be a mediator between the living and the dead. The funeral lament has a twofold ritual function: to secure the safe passage of the deceased from this world to the next, and to provide him with a message to pass on to the ancestors. Here is a fragment from a Serbian lament:

> So I beseech you in pain,
> To waste no time when you get there
> In greeting our many cousins
> Whom we buried before you.
> Tell them, master, truthfully,
> That we are in pain and sorrow
> Because they don't remember us.
> They don't visit their old homestead,
> They don't ask others about us.[25]

Now I will demonstrate how the oral tradition preserves in its memory the connection between the cult of the dead, the funeral lament and the secular ballad.

In certain ballads of the Balkan tradition – Serbo-Croatian, Rumanian and Greek – we notice a very peculiar way of describing the death of the protagonist. In the sixteenth-century ballad of *Marko and Andrijaš*, Marko mortally wounds his brother. In a touching piece of irony Andrijaš, dying, instructs Marko on how he is to explain to their mother why Andrijaš will never return home:

Say: the hero has remained in a foreign land, dear mother,
Which he cannot leave because of its charms . . .
He has fallen in love with a pretty maiden . . .
She gave him many strange herbs
And that wine of forgetfulness, the pretty maiden.[26]

In another ballad[27], a father attending the funeral of his two daughters, dead of the plague, says that they have gone to their wedding. The identification of the two events – death and marriage – and the two ceremonies – funeral and wedding – has the effect of creating emotional tension and irony.

In funeral laments, the deceased is described as preparing for his wedding. One explanation for this metaphor lies in the fact that, according to their ritual function, these songs are not supposed to mention death. They avoid mentioning it by saying that the deceased is 'leaving', preparing for 'a journey', moving to another 'home' where he will 'join another of his kin'. A second explanation lies in the deep connection between death and rebirth, between passing away and getting married, because the latter implies a similar procedure: the bride is to leave her parents' house, she is going on a journey, she is moving to a new home and becoming a member of another kin group. Both events, therefore, imply mediating between two classes of kin: the living and the dead, or the bride's family and the groom's. This is the point of contact between funeral and wedding laments. The oral tradition has preserved this point in its memory. Here is an example of a wedding lament:

> Quiet now, don't weep, dear maiden heart,
> Your mother will weep her fill for you,
> Will weep her fill, will mourn you.
> When the girls go to fetch water
> There will be no lovely Ruža at the spring,
> No lovely Ruža, no cool water.[28]

Wedding laments such as this one are sung exclusively at the moment the bride is 'taken away' from the parents' house. All the other songs associated with the wedding ceremony are joyful. But I must mention that laughter – strange as this may sound – is also associated with death. Ethnologists have noticed that laughter and merry-making were customary in the cult of the dead, and not only customary but obligatory during the wake for the deceased, and at the graveside ritual (the *daća*). We have an example of this preserved in the folk song 'The death of King Uroš'. When the mother hears that her young son has been killed, she goes to the grave and starts 'laughing loudly'.[29] All this would seem quite cynical if we were to forget that laughter in these situations is a ritual act, supposed to assist the soul of the dead man and protect him from evil spirits at this critical moment, when he is most susceptible to their influence.

Ritual folk songs show that the information preserved by oral tradition is not only a factor of continuity, stability and identity, but is also an instrument of protection as well as a means of mastering, even of overpowering, the time dimension of life – the distinction between past and present, between dead ancestors and living descendants.

The Sephardic tradition in Yugoslavia

Finally, I would like to present a special case of memory involving the oral tradition. It concerns the Jewish people, specifically the Spanish Jews or Sephardim.

The Jewish presence in Spain dates from the beginning of our era. The Moslem dominance of the Spanish lands witnessed the development of a great literary tradition in the Hebrew language. In the late Middle Ages, however, a deep historical change brought about the Hispanicization of the Jews, a process which was well underway at the time of their expulsion in 1492, the year the *reconquista* was concluded. Most of the exiles settled in Turkish territories along the African coast, in the Near East and the Balkans. Since cultural assimilation had been going on for quite a long time prior to their expulsion, Judaeo-Spanish was the everyday colloquial language of the exiles, as well as the language of their oral tradition. Therefore, the secular oral culture of the Sephardim was based on the Spanish language and the tradition encoded in it. Hebrew was preserved as the holy language associated with liturgy, education and religious literature. The culture of the Sephardim, therefore, involved two different traditions: one secular and basically Spanish, the other thoroughly Jewish and religious, in the broadest sense of the word.

Post-exile Sephardic oral culture is an astonishing example of memory preserving both Jewish content and Spanish forms.[30] When M. Manrique de Lara, a Spanish scholar, visited Belgrade in 1911 he was surprised to hear Jews not only speaking the Judaeo-Spanish language, but singing an old song long forgotten in Spain. It was about a king on his deathbed:

> El buen rey esta hazino / di dulor di corazon,
> ya mandan por los dotores / cuantos en el mundo son . . .[31]

Some of these lines were very similar to those in a fifteenth-century text of the romance *Morirse quiere Aleixandre*, a Spanish ballad popular before the expulsion of the Jews. Later it was completely forgotten in the Peninsular tradition, but preserved among the Jews in Belgrade up to the twentieth century. Many other songs of Spanish origin, especially those dealing with protagonists and events from Spanish history, were suppressed from the Sephardic *romancero*, while others were preserved, but with their historical layer obliterated. Such is the case of the ballad on the death in 1497 of Prince Juan, son of the Spanish rulers Fernando and Isabella. The Spanish tradition has preserved the ballad as well as the historical details it contains, while the Sephardic tradition has been ambiguous in its memory – preserving the song, but not its historical content. The Judaeo-Spanish versions collected in North Africa are about a man on his deathbed – any man or every man. And since it has become a song on death itself, it has gradually changed its form and function, turning into a sort of lament.[32]

A similar case is presented by a number of old Sephardic songs from Spain, as well as more recent ones created and traditional-ized among the Sephardim in the Balkans, songs dealing with protagonists and events from Jewish history. The themes are Jewish, but the forms are basically Spanish. The Sephardic tradition has obviously preserved the Spanish heritage as an instrument for expressing Jewish traditional cultural values.

We have already seen that memory manifests itself in oral tradition in a very complex way. I will now present a few examples, showing one more level of the memory mechanism 'ticking' inside the oral tradition. They illustrate the use of allegorical interpretation as a means of Judaicization.

The 'Complas de Tubishevat' or 'Songs of fruits and flowers' were created among the Spanish Jews after exile from Spain and traditionalized subsequently by oral transmission. They are sung on the fifteenth day of the month of *shevat*, which is mentioned in the Talmud as the day celebrating the rebirth of nature in the Holy Land. Tubishevat is not a religious holiday. But among the Sephardim, since the eighteenth century at least, it was celebrated mainly as a reminiscence of the Holy Land by the people in exile. It is interesting to note that this holiday occurs in February, which in the Balkans is a winter month, when there are no signs whatsoever of the rebirth of nature.(The Balkan peoples have similar holidays celebrating spring, such as St. George's Day, but they fall in April or May.) As a sort of fertility ritual, Tubishevat implies a parallelism between the natural world and the community of the Jews, one emphasized by the reference to the Holy Land. Thus the rebirth of nature is interpreted as an allegory of the rebirth of the Jewish people and their return to Israel. Since the Tubishevat songs speak of all the fruits of nature, they are first a praise to God's creation. Next, they are an expression of the yearning of the exiles to return to the Holy Land. Thirdly, they contain details concerning widespread folk beliefs.

The main part of these songs consists of a competition of personified flowers or fruits, in which each one speaks of its beauty and power. Songs containing a similar competition pattern are well known in the tradition of the Balkan peoples, and it is quite possible that the model of these songs could have been taken from Balkan sources.[33] But the Serbian song of the same type is associated with an obvious lyrical theme – love – and has an obviously erotic meaning, while the Sephardic versions effect an allegorical reinterpretation which turns them into a praise to God's creation and a hymn to the Holy Land.

The same procedure was applied to some songs of Spanish origin. Such is the case with the essentially non-religious ballad 'La tormenta calmada', which in the Sephardic reinterpretation has come to 'celebrate in the most fervent terms God's miraculous response to the prayers of a true believer'.[34]

The seventeenth and eighteenth centuries were times when messianic ideas were widespread among the Balkan Sephardim, times which brought forth a false messiah called Shabetay Zevi, who ended his career by converting to Islam. But before this happened, he became famous for his sermons which concluded with the singing of an old Spanish love song describing a beautiful girl, Melisenda, as she is coming out of the river after bathing. This secular love song, performed in this context, was reinterpreted in a specific way: the beautiful lady is identified with the Jewish people, the 'bride' coming out of the ritual bath and preparing for the coming of the Messiah.[35]

How is this connected with memory?

One of the prominent features of the Jewish cultural tradition is the allegorical interpretation of sacred texts. An opening line of The Song of Solomon reads: 'Because of the savour of thy good ointments thy name is as ointment poured forth, therefore do the virgins love thee.'[36] Allegory is the means whereby *ointment* is interpreted as knowledge and wisdom of the Torah. Without allegory this love song, with its erotic overtones and celebration of fertility, could not be included in the Holy Scripture. In the case of the above Spanish love song, the same interpretative code is used to carry out the Judaicization of the text and this is certainly a factor providing for the preservation of the song in the Sephardic tradition. Thus the memory of an old song, The Song of Solomon, influences the preservation of a new one, with the condition that it be reinterpreted in a specific way. And in this way the memory of the Holy Land influences the creation of new songs expressing hope in the future.

As for the Sephardim, we can distinguish three phases of development. First, there took place the assimilation in Spain, whereby a particular Judaeo-Spanish cultural model was perfected in the oral tradition. Secondly, there ensued a four-century-long phase during which this model was preserved. Thirdly, a new cultural model was created, following a deep crisis of identity.

The Judaeo-Spanish language in the Balkans had for centuries been confined to Sephardic communities isolated from the Slavic cultural environment. This kind of isolation was impossible to maintain in the twentieth century. Integration in the social and economic life of the country meant accepting the Serbo-Croatian language, and this implied adopting the tradition – oral as well as written – encoded in this language. Although a similar process of assimilation had been carried out in Spain before their expulsion, the Sephardim felt that the loss of the Judaeo-Spanish language meant the loss of Sephardic cultural identity. However, the conditions under which this second process of assimilation took place in the Balkans were radically different in at least two ways: first, the written and printed word had imposed itself as the dominant form of communication; and secondly, the overall role of religion had changed. But the most important factor in terms of memory was isolation. On the one hand, it had enabled the long preservation of the Judaeo-Spanish cultural model; but on the other, it caused its gradual fossilization and decay.

In conclusion, I would like to point out that it is common knowledge that the tremendous system of oral lore that once existed in Yugoslavia – the epic songs, the ballads, the tales and ritual songs – has been dying out for a long time. What is noteworthy, however, is not what has disappeared from the mouths of our peasants, but what has been retained – transformed at times, but still surviving. Folklore survives in our everyday speech. Yugoslavs are fond of proverbs and sayings – not only those of the Bible, but also of our favourite poets, including the great nineteenth-century poet Njegoš, who represents the transition from an oral culture to written literature. Graveside rituals and, to some extent, wedding rituals still survive as well, in a perhaps more simplified form. Even today children learn fairy tales before they learn to read and write. Thus oral culture continues to exist together with the written, both of them created by memory – the author of the Book of the Universe.

Notes

1 J. M. Lotman y Escuela de Tartu, *Semiótica de la cultura*, Madrid, 1979.

2 For more on the relationship between the oral and the written Gospels, see Werner H. Kelber's *The Oral and Written Gospel: The Hermeneutics of Speaking and Writing in the Synoptic Tradition, Mark, Paul and Q*, Philadelphia: Fortress Press, 1983. See also *Q: The Sayings of Jesus*, by Ivan Havener, OSB, with a reconstruction of Q by Athanasius Polag, Good News Studies no. 19, Wilmington, Del.: Michael Glazier.

3 For more on the use of the formula in oral composition, see Albert B. Lord's *The Singer of Tales*, Cambridge, Mass., 1960.

4 Matthew 26:34; Mark 14:30; Luke 22:34; John 13:38.

5 V. J. Propp, *Morfologija skazki*, Leningrad, 1928.

6 V. Karadžić, *Srpske narodne pjesme*, vol. 2, Belgrade, 1969, no. 48, 'Smrt majke Jugovića'.

7 J. Tomić, *Rat na Kosovu i Staroj Srbiji 1912 godine*, Novi Sad, 1913, p. 120.

8 D. Pavlović and R. Marinković, *Iz naše književnosti feudalnog doba*, Sarajevo, 1954, pp. 136–8.

9 V. Karadžić, ibid., vol. 2, no. 46, 'Propast carstva srpskoga', tr. T. Butler.

10 V. Karadžić, ibid., vol. 2, no. 50, 'Komadi od različnijeh kosovskijeh pjesama', tr. T. Butler.

11 V. Karadžić, ibid., vol. 2, no. 53, 'Obretenije glave kneza Lazara', tr. T. Butler.

12 V. J. Propp, *Istoričeskie korni volšebnoj skazki*, Leningrad, 1946.

13 F. J. Child, *The English and Scottish Popular Ballads*, vol. 1, Boston, 1882–1898, no. 17.

14 V. Karadžić, ibid., vol. 3, no. 25, 'Ropstvo Janković Stojana'; B. Desnica, 'Ropstvo Janković Stojana (istorijska osnova Vukove pesme, III, br. 25)', *Prilozi za književnost, jezik, istoriju i folklor*, 2 (1922), pp. 196–200.

15 Cf. bibliography in N. Ljubinković, 'Legenda o Vladimiru i Kosari (Izmedju pisane i usmene književnosti)', *MSC*, 2 (Belgrade, 1977), pp. 139–45.

16 F. Šišić, *Letopis popa Dukljanina*, Belgrade and Zagreb, 1928.

17 A. Kačić-Miošić, 'Pisma od kralja Vladimira', *Razgovor ugodni naroda slovinskoga*, Pet stoljeća hrvatske književnosti, vol. 21, Zagreb, 1967, pp. 55–9.

18 Cf. T. Maretić, *Naša narodna epika*, Belgrade, 1966, pp. 25–6, 288.
19 V. Karadžić, ibid., vol. 2, no. 64, 'Marko Kraljević i kći kralja arapskoga'.
20 V. Karadžić, ibid., vol. 3, no. 21, 'Ženidba Stojana Jankovića'.
21 Maretić, ibid., pp. 289–90, 348.
22 V. Čajkanović, *Mit i religija u Srba. Izabrane studije*, ed. V. Djurić, Belgrade, 1973, pp. 126, 194.
23 Ibid., pp. 295–303.
24 Ibid., pp. 169–79.
25 V. Karadžić, ibid., vol. 1, no. 151, 'Kad mrtvaca iznesu iz kuće', tr. T. Butler.
26 *Bugarštice*, ed. N. Kilibarda, Belgrade, 1979, pp. 50–2, tr. T. Butler.
27 H. Krnjević, *Usmene balade Bosne i Hercegovine*, Sarajevo, 1973, p. 401.
28 V. Karadžić, ibid., vol. 1, no. 42, 'Kad izvedu djevojku', tr. T. Butler.
29 V. Čajkanović, ibid., pp. 100–1, 108–27.
30 K. Vidaković Petrov, *Kultura španskih Jevreja na jugoslovenskom tlu*, Sarajevo, 1986.
31 M. Manrique de Lara, 'Romances españoles en los Balkanes', *Blanco y Negro*, 1916, no. 1285.
32 P. Bénichou, *Creación poética en el romancero tradicional*, Madrid, 1968, pp. 95–124.
33 S. G. Armistead and J. Silverman, 'Las "Complas de las flores" y la poesía popular de los Balkanes', *Sefarad*, 28 (1968).
34 S. G. Armistead and J. Silverman, *The Judaeo-Spanish Ballad Chapbooks of Y. A. Yoná*, University of California Press, 1971, p. 280.
35 R. Menéndez Pidal, 'Un viejo romance cantado por Sabbatai Cevi', *De primitiva lírica española y antigua épica*, Madrid, 1968, pp. 93–6.
36 The Song of Solomon 1:3.

5

History as Social Memory
Peter Burke

The traditional view of the relation between history and memory is a relatively simple one. The historian's function is to be a 'remembrancer', the custodian of the memory of public events which are put down in writing for the benefit of the actors, to give them fame, and also for the benefit of posterity, to learn from their example. History, as Cicero wrote in a passage which has been quoted ever since, is 'the life of memory' (*vita memoriae*).[1] Historians as diverse as Herodotus, Froissart and Lord Clarendon, all claimed to write in order to keep alive the memory of great deeds and great events. Two Byzantine historians made the point particularly fully in their prologues, utilizing the traditional metaphors of time as a river and of actions as texts which may be obliterated. Anna Comnena described history as a 'bulwark' against the 'stream of time' which carries everything away into 'the depths of oblivion', while Procopius declared that he wrote his history of the Gothic, Persian and other wars 'to the end that the long course of time may not overwhelm deeds of singular importance through lack of a record, and thus abandon them to oblivion and utterly obliterate them'.[2] The idea of actions as texts can also be seen in the notion of the 'book of memory', employed by Dante and Shakespeare, who wrote of 'blotting your name from books of memory'.[3]

This traditional account of the relation between memory and written history, in which memory reflects what actually happened and history reflects memory, now seems rather too simple. Both history and memory are coming to appear increasingly problematic. Remembering the past and writing about it no longer seem the innocent activities they were once taken to be. Neither memories nor histories seem objective any longer. In both cases we are learning to take account of conscious or unconscious selection, interpretation and distortion. In both cases this selection, interpretation and distortion is socially conditioned. It is not the work of individuals alone.

The first serious explorer of the 'social framework of memory', as he called it, was the French sociologist Maurice Halbwachs in the 1920s.[4] Halbwachs argued that memories are constructed by social groups. Individuals remember, in the literal, physical sense. However, it is social groups which determine what is 'memorable' and also how it will be remembered. Individuals identify with public events of importance to their group. They 'remember' a good deal that they have not experienced directly. A news item, for example, can be an event in itself, an event which becomes part of one's life.

A faithful pupil of Emile Durkheim, Halbwachs couched his arguments about the sociology of memory in a strong if not an extreme form. Halbwachs did not assert (as the Cambridge psychologist Frederick Bartlett accused him of doing), that social groups remember in the same literal sense that individuals remember.[5] However, Halbwachs *was* vulnerable to the more precise criticisms of the great French historian Marc Bloch, who pointed out the danger of borrowing terms from individual psychology and simply adding the adjective 'collective' (as in the cases of *représentations collectives*, *mentalités collectives*, *conscience collective*, as well as *mémoire collective*).[6] All the same, Bloch was prepared to adopt the phrase *mémoire collective* and to analyse peasant customs in these interdisciplinary terms, noting for example the importance of grandparents in the transmission of traditions.[7]

Halbwachs made a sharp distinction between collective memory, which was a social construct, and written history, which he considered – in a somewhat old-fashioned positivist way – to be objective. However, current studies of the history of historical writing treat it much as Halbwachs treated memory, as the product of social groups such as Roman senators, Chinese mandarins, Benedictine monks, university professors and so on.

It is becoming commonplace to point out that in different places and times, historians have considered different aspects of the past to be memorable (battles, politics, religion, the economy and so on) and that they have presented the past in very different ways (concentrating on events or structures, on great men or ordinary people, according to their group's point of view).

It is because I share this latter, relativist view of the history of history that I chose the title 'history as social memory' for this piece, using the term as a convenient piece of shorthand which sums up the complex process of selection and interpretation in a simple formula and stresses the homology between the ways in which the past is recorded and remembered.[8]

The phrase 'social memory' and the term 'relativism' do raise awkard problems, so I had better try to state my position, as follows. The analogies between individual and group thought are as elusive as they are fascinating. If we use terms like 'social memory' we do risk reifying concepts. On the other hand, if we refuse to use such terms, we are in danger of failing to notice the different ways in which the ideas of individuals are influenced by the groups to which they belong. As for historical relativism, my argument is not that any account of the past is just as good (reliable, plausible, perceptive . . .) as any other; some investigators are better-informed or more judicious than others. The point is that we have access to the past (like the present) only via the categories and schemata (or as Durkheim would say, the 'collective representations') of our own culture.

At this point it may be possible to redefine the place of history in this interdisciplinary series of essays. Historians are concerned, or at any rate need to be concerned, with memory from two different points of view. In the first place, they need to study memory as a historical *source*, to produce a critique of the reliability of reminiscence on the lines of the traditional critique of historical documents. This enterprise has in fact been under way since the 1960s, when historians of the twentieth century came to realize the importance of 'oral history'.[9] Even those of us who work on earlier periods have something to learn from the oral history movement, since we need to be aware of the oral testimonies and traditions embedded in many written records.[10]

In the second place, historians are concerned, or should be concerned, with memory as a historical phenomenon; with what might be called the social history of remembering. Given the fact that the social memory, like the individual memory, is selective, we need to identify the principles of selection and to note how they vary from place to place or from one group to another and how they change over time. Memories are malleable, and we need to understand how they are shaped and by whom. These are topics which for some reason attracted the attention of historians only in the late 1970s; but now there seem to be books and articles and conferences about them everywhere.[11]

It is this second topic, the social history of remembering, on which I should like to concentrate, dividing it into three main sections or questions.

1 What are the modes of transmission of public memories and how have these modes changed over time?
2 What are the uses of these memories, the uses of the past, and how have these uses changed?
3 Conversely, what are the uses of oblivion?

Huge questions: but I shall be looking at them from the relatively narrow point of view of a historian of early modern Europe, concentrating on written traditions rather than oral ones and on 'documents' rather than 'literature' to avoid overlapping with other contributors to this volume. As we shall soon see, however, these dichotomies are very far from clear or distinct.

Transmission of the social memory

Memories are affected by the social organization of transmission and the different media employed. Consider for a moment the sheer variety of these media, five in particular.

1   Oral traditions, discussed from a historian's point of view in a famous study by Jan Vansina. The transformations of this study make useful indicators of the changes which have taken place in the discipline of history in the last generation, notably the decline of positivism and the rise of interest in symbolic aspects of narrative.[12]

2   The traditional province of the historian, memoirs and other written records (another term related to remembering, *ricordare* in Italian). We need of course to remind ourselves, as historians often do, that these records are not innocent acts of memory, but rather attempts to persuade, to shape the memory of others. We also need to keep in mind, as historians have not always done, the warning of a perceptive literary critic, the sinologist Stephen Owen: 'As we read the writings of memory, it is easy to forget that we do not read memory itself but its transformation through writing.'[13]

3   Images, pictorial or photographic, still or moving. Practitioners of the so-called 'art of memory', from classical antiquity to the Renaissance, emphasized the value of associating whatever one wanted to remember with striking images.[14] These were immaterial, indeed 'imaginary images': but material images have long been constructed in order to assist the retention and transmission of memories – 'memorials' such as tombstones, statues, and medals, and 'souvenirs' of various kinds. Historians of the nineteenth and twentieth centuries in particular have been taking an increasing interest in public monuments in the last few years, precisely because these monuments both expressed and shaped the national memory.[15]

4   Actions transmit memories as they transmit skills, from master to apprentice for example. Many of them leave no traces for later historians to study but ritual actions in particular are often recorded, including rituals of 'commemoration': Remembrance Sunday in Britain, Memorial Day in the USA, 14 July in France, 12 July in Northern Ireland.[16] These rituals are re-enactments of the past, acts of memory, but they are also attempts to impose interpretations of the past, to shape memory. They are in every sense collective re-presentations.

5   One of the most interesting observations in the study of the social framework of memory by Maurice Halbwachs concerned the importance of a fifth medium in the transmission of memories: space. He made explicit a point implicit in the classical and Renaissance art of memory; the value of 'placing' images that one wishes to remember in particular locations such as memory palaces or memory theatres. Some of the Catholic missionaries in

Brazil, the Salesian Fathers, were apparently aware of the link between spaces and memories. One of their strategies for the conversion of the Bororo Indians, as Lévi-Strauss reminds us, was to move them from their traditional villages, in which houses were arranged in a circle, to new ones in which the houses were arranged in rows, thus wiping the slate clean and making it ready to receive the Christian message.[17]

I sometimes wonder whether the European enclosure movement may not have had similar effects (however unintentional) in wiping the slate clean for industrialization. Especially in Sweden, where the destruction of traditional villages and their relocation was even more complete than in England.[18]

Yet in certain circumstances, a social group and some of its memories may resist the destruction of its home.[19] An extreme example of uprooting and transplantation is the case of the black slaves transported to the New World. Despite this uprooting, the slaves were able to cling to some of their culture, some of their memories, and to reconstruct it on American soil. According to one of its leading interpreters, the ritual of *candomblé*, still widely practised in Brazil, involves a symbolic reconstruction of African space, a kind of psychological compensation for the loss of a homeland.[20]

From the point of view of the transmission of memories each medium has its own strengths and weaknesses. But I should like to place most emphasis on something which is common to several media, and has been analysed by investigators as different as the social psychologist Frederick Bartlett, the cultural historian Aby Warburg, and the Slavist Albert Lord: and that is the 'schema', associated with the tendency to represent (or indeed to remember) one event or one person in terms of another.[21]

However, schemata of this kind are not confined to oral traditions, as the following chain of written examples may suggest. In his fine study *The Great War and Modern Memory*, the American critic Paul Fussell has noted what he calls 'the domination of the Second War by the First', not only at the level of the generals, who are supposed always to be fighting the previous war, but at the level of ordinary participants as well.[22]

The First World War was also perceived in terms of schemata, and Fussell notes the recurrence of imagery from Bunyan's *Pilgrim's Progress*, especially the Slough of Despond and the Valley of the Shadow of Death, in descriptions of life in the trenches in memoirs and newspapers.[23] To go back a little further, Bunyan's own writing – including his autobiography, *Grace Abounding* – also made use of schemata; Bunyan's account of his conversion is clearly modelled, consciously or unconsciously – it is difficult to say which – on the conversion of St. Paul as described in the *Acts of the Apostles*.[24]

In early modern Europe, many people had read the Bible so often that it had become part of them and its stories organized their perceptions and their memories. It would not be difficult to cite scores of examples of this process, such as the following. Johann Kessler was a Swiss Protestant pastor of the first generation. In his memoirs he tells the story of how, as he puts it, 'Martin Luther met me on the road to Wittenberg'. He and a companion stayed the night in the Black Bear at Jena, where they shared a table with a man who was dressed as a knight but was reading a book – which turned out to be a Hebrew psalter – and prepared to talk about theology. 'We asked, "Sir, can you tell us whether Dr Martin Luther is in Wittenberg just now, or where else he may be?" He replied, "I know for certain that he is not at Wittenberg at this moment". . . . "My boys," he asked, "what do they think about this Luther in Switzerland?"' The students still don't get the point until the landlord drops a hint.[25] My own point, however, is that consciously or unconsciously, Kessler has structured his story on a biblical prototype, that of the disciples who met Christ on the road to Emmaus.

The chain of examples could be stretched still further back, since the Bible itself is full of schemata, and some of the events narrated in it are presented as re-enactments of earlier ones.[26] However, the examples already given are perhaps sufficient to suggest some features of the process by which the remembered past turns into myth. I am, incidentally, using that slippery term 'myth' not in the positivist sense of 'inaccurate history' but in the richer, more positive sense of a story with a symbolic meaning, made up of stereotyped incidents and involving characters who are larger than life, whether they are heroes or villains.

There is an obvious question for a historian to ask at this point. Why do myths attach themselves to some individuals (living or dead) and not to others? Only a few rulers have become heroes in popular memory; Henry IV of France, for example, William III of England, Frederick the Great. It is not every holy man or woman who becomes a saint, official or unofficial. Why? The existence of oral or literary schemata, or more generally of perceptual schemata, does not explain why these schemata become attached to particular individuals, why some people are, shall we say, more 'mythogenic' than others. Nor is it an adequate answer to do what literal-minded positivist historians generally do and describe the actual achievements of the successful rulers or saints, considerable as these may be, since the myth often attributes qualities to them which there is no evidence that they ever possessed.[27] The transformation of the cold and colourless William III into the popular Protestant idol 'King Billy' can hardly be explained in terms of his own personality.

In my view, the central element in the explanation of this mythogenesis is the perception (conscious or unconscious) of a 'fit' in some respect or respects between a particular individual and a current stereotype of a hero or villain – ruler, saint, bandit, witch, or whatever. This 'fit' strikes people's imagination and stories about that individual begin to circulate, orally in the first instance. In the course of this oral circulation, the ordinary mechanisms of distortion studied by social psychologists, such as 'levelling' and 'sharpening', come into play. These mechanisms assist the assimilation of the life of the particular individual to a particular stereotype from the repertoire of stereotypes present in the social memory in a given culture.[28] Bandits turn into Robin Hoods, robbing the rich to give to the poor. Rulers travel their kingdom in disguise to learn about the condition of their subjects. The life of a modern saint may be remembered as a re-enactment of the life of an earlier one: St. Carlo Borromeo was perceived as a second Ambrose, and St. Rose of Lima as a second Catherine of Siena. William III of England was perceived as a second William the Conqueror.

But of course this explanation of the process of hero-making in terms of the media is insufficient. To offer it as a complete explanation would be politically naive. I have still to consider the function of the social memory.

Uses of the social memory

What is the function of the social memory? It is hard to get a purchase on such a large question. If a lawyer was contributing to this series of lectures, he or she might well discuss the importance of custom and precedent, the justification or legitimation of actions in the present with reference to the past, the function of the memories of witnesses in courts of law, the concept of 'time immemorial', in other words time 'whereof the memory of man . . . runneth not to the contrary', and the change in attitudes to the evidence of memory consequent on the spread of literacy and written records.[29]

As a cultural historian, I find it helpful to approach the question of the uses of social memory by asking why some cultures seem to be more concerned with recalling their past than others. It is commonplace to contrast the traditional Chinese concern for their past with the traditional Indian indifference to theirs. Within Europe, contrasts of this kind are also apparent. Despite their reverence for tradition and concern for 'the national heritage', to be discussed by Patrick Wright, the social memory of the English is relatively short. The Irish and the Poles, on the other hand, have social memories which are relatively long. On a visit to Belfast, in 1969, I remember seeing a portrait of William III on horseback, chalked on a wall, with the inscription, 'Remember 1690'. In the South of Ireland, people still resent what the English did to them in Cromwell's time as if it were yesterday. In Poland, Andrzej Wajda's film *Ashes*, set in the era of Napoleon, provoked national controversy about what Wajda seemed to view as the futile heroism of the Polish Legion. Here, on the other hand, at much the same time, the film *The Charge of the Light Brigade* was treated as little more than a costume picture. The English seem to prefer to forget.[30] They suffer from, or rejoice in, what the social anthropologist John Barnes has called

'structural amnesia'.[31] Since structural amnesia is the comple-
mentary opposite to the concept 'social memory', I shall re-
christen it 'social amnesia'.

Why is there such a sharp contrast in attitudes to the past in
different cultures? It is often said that history is written by the
victors. It might also be said that history is forgotten by the
victors. They can afford to forget, while the losers are unable to
accept what happened and are condemned to brood over it, relive
it, and reflect how different it might have been. Another
explanation might be given in terms of cultural roots. When you
have them you can afford to take them for granted but when you
lose them you search for them. The Irish and the Poles have been
uprooted, their countries partitioned; it is no wonder they seem
obsessed by their past. We have returned to that favourite theme
of Halbwachs, the relation between place and memory.

The Irish and the Poles offer particularly clear examples of the
use of the past, the use of the social memory, and the use of
myth in order to define identity. The point of remembering 1690
(in a particular way), or re-enacting the 12 July, or blowing up
Nelson's Pillar – as the IRA did in 1966 – or of reconstructing the
old centre of Warsaw, after the Germans had blown it up – as the
Poles did after 1945 – the point of all this is surely to say who
'we' are, and to distinguish 'us' from them. Such examples could
be multiplied. In the case of Europe, they are particularly easy to
find in the nineteenth century.

The later nineteenth century has been provocatively described
as the age of the 'invention of tradition'.[32] It was certainly an age
of a search for national traditions, in which national monuments
were constructed, and national rituals (like Bastille Day) devised,
while national history had a greater place in European schools
than ever before or since. The aim of all this was essentially to
justify or 'legitimate' the existence of the nation-state; whether
in the case of new nations like Italy and Germany, or of older
ones like France, in which national loyalty still had to be created,
and peasants turned into Frenchmen.[33]

The sociology of Emile Durkheim, with its emphasis on
community, consensus and cohesion, itself bears the stamp of
this period. It would be unwise to follow Durkheim and his

pupil Halbwachs too closely in this respect, and to discuss the social function of the social memory as if conflict and dissent did not exist. I have referred to Northern Ireland several times already and it is a classic example, though far from the only one, of both memories of conflict and conflicts of memory.[34] Given the multiplicity of social identities, and the coexistence of rival memories, alternative memories (family memories, local memories, class memories, national memories, and so on), it is surely more fruitful to think in pluralistic terms about the uses of memories to different social groups, who may well have different views about what is significant or 'worthy of memory'.[35]

The American literary critic Stanley Fish coined the phrase 'interpretative communities' in order to analyse conflicts over the interpretation of texts. In a similar way, it might be useful to think in terms of different 'memory communities' within a given society. It is important to ask the question, who wants whom to remember what, and why? Whose version of the past is recorded and preserved?

Disputes between historians presenting rival accounts of the past sometimes reflect wider and deeper social conflicts. An obvious example is the current debate about the importance of history from below, a debate which goes back at least as far as Aleksandr Pushkin, a historian as well as a poet, who told the tsar that he wanted to write about the eighteenth-century peasant leader Pugachev. The tsar's reply was brutally simple: 'such a man has no history'.

Official and unofficial memories of the past may differ sharply and the unofficial memories, which have been relatively little studied, are sometimes historical forces in their own right; the 'Good Old Law' in the German Peasant War of 1525, the 'Norman Yoke' in the English Revolution, and so on. Without invoking social memories of this kind, it would be hard to explain the geography of dissent and protest, the fact that some villages, for example, take part in different protest movements century after century, while others do not.

The systematic destruction of documents which is such a common feature of revolts – think of the English peasants in

1381, the German peasants in 1525, the French peasants in 1789, and so on – may be interpreted as the expression of the belief that the records had falsified the situation, that they were biased in favour of the ruling class, while ordinary people remembered what had really happened. These acts of destruction broach my last topic, the uses of oblivion or social amnesia.

The uses of social amnesia

It is often illuminating to approach problems from behind, to turn them inside out. To understand the workings of the social memory it may be worth investigating the social organization of forgetting, the rules of exclusion, suppression or repression, and the question of who wants whom to forget what, and why. Amnesia is related to 'amnesty', to what used to be called 'acts of oblivion', official erasure of memories of conflict in the interests of social cohesion.

Official censorship of the past is all too well known, and there is little need to talk about the various revisions of the *Soviet Encyclopaedia*. Many revolutionary and counter-revolutionary regimes like to symbolize their break with the past by changing the names of streets, especially when these names refer to the dates of significant events. When I visited Bulgaria in the mid-1960s, the only guidebook I had with me was a *Guide Bleu* of 1938. Despite the street-maps it provided I sometimes lost my way, and so I had to ask passers-by how to find 12 November street, or whatever it was. No one looked surprised, no one smiled, they simply directed me, but when I arrived, 12 November street turned out to be 1 May street, and so on. This incident may be taken as an encouraging reminder of the strength of unofficial memories and the difficulty of erasing them, even under the so-called 'totalitarian' regimes of our own day.

As it happens, what might be called the '*Soviet Encyclopaedia* syndrome' is not the invention of such regimes. In early modern Europe too, events could become non-events, officially at least. King Louis XIV and his advisers were very much concerned with what we would call his 'public image'. Medals were struck to commemorate the major events of the reign including the destruction of the city of Heidelberg in 1693. However, when the medals were collected together to form a 'metallic history' of the reign, this particular medal disappeared from the catalogue. It seems that Louis had come to realize that the destruction of Heidelberg had not added to his reputation, his glory, and so the event was officially suppressed, erased from the book of memory.[36]

The official censorship of embarrassing memories is well known. What is in need of investigation is their unofficial suppression or repression, and this topic raises once more the awkward question of the analogy between individual and collective memory. Freud's famous metaphor of the 'censor' inside each individual was of course derived from the official censorship of the Habsburg Empire. In a similar manner, a social psychologist, Peter Berger, has suggested that we all rewrite our biographies all the time in the manner of the *Soviet Encyclopaedia*.[37] But between these two censors, public and private, there is space for a third, collective but unofficial. Can groups, like individuals, suppress what it is inconvenient to remember? If so, how do they do it?[38]

Consider the following story, recorded by the anthropologist Jack Goody. The origin of the territorial divisions of Gonja, in northern Ghana, was said to have been the act of the founder, Jakpa, who divided the kingdom among his sons. 'When the details of this story were first recorded at the turn of the present century, at the time that the British were extending their control over the area, Jakpa was said to have begotten seven sons, this corresponding to the number of divisions. . . . But at the same time as the British had arrived, two of the seven divisions disappeared . . . sixty years later, when the myths of state were again recorded, Jakpa was credited with only five sons.'[39] This is a classic case of the past being used to legitimate the present, of what Malinowski described as myth functioning as the 'charter' of institutions (borrowing the term 'charter' from the historians of the Middle Ages).

I would not care to assert that this adjustment of the past to the present is to be found only in societies without writing. Indeed, it is often quite easy to show major discrepancies between the image of the past shared by members of a particular social group, and the surviving records of that past. A recurrent myth (to be found in many forms in our own society today) is that of the 'founding fathers'; the story of Martin Luther founding the Protestant church, of Emile Durkheim (or Max Weber) founding sociology, and so on. Generally speaking, what happens in the case of these myths is that differences between past and present are elided, and unintended consequences are turned into conscious aims, as if the main purpose of these past heroes had been to bring about the present – our present.

Writing and print are not powerful enough to stop the spread of myths of this kind. What they can do, however, is to preserve records of the past which are inconsistent with the myths, which undermine them – records of a past which has become awkward and embarrassing, a past which people for one reason or another do not wish to know about, though it might be better for them if they did. It might, for example, free them from the dangerous illusion that past, present and future may be seen as a simple struggle between heroes and villains, good and evil, right and wrong. Myths are not to be despised, but reading them literally is not to be recommended.

Herodotus thought of historians as the guardians of memory, the memory of glorious deeds. I prefer to see historians as the guardians of awkward facts, the skeletons in the cupboard of the social memory.[40] There used to be an official called the 'Remembrancer'. The title was actually a euphemism for debt-collector; the official's job was to remind people of what they would have liked to forget. One of the most important functions of the historian is to be a remembrancer.

Notes

1 Cicero, *De oratore*, 2. 36.
2 Procopius, *De bellis*, ed. H. W. Dewy, London and New York, 1914, p. 1.
3 *2 Henry VI*, I. i.

4 M. Halbwachs, *Les cadres sociaux de la mémoire*, Paris, 1925. Cf. D. Lowenthal, *The Past is a Foreign Country*, Cambridge, 1985, pp. 192 f.

5 F. C. Bartlett, *Remembering: a Study in Experimental and Social Psychology*, Cambridge, 1932, pp. 296 f. A similar misunderstanding of a Durkheimian position is shown by those British historians who believe that the 'collective mentalities' studied by their French colleagues stand outside individuals rather than being shared by them. Halbwachs is defended against Bartlett by Mary Douglas in her introduction to the English translation of his *Collective Memory*, New York, 1980.

6 M. Bloch, 'Mémoire collective, tradition et coutume', *Revue de Synthèse Historique*, 40 (1925), pp. 73–83.

7 Ibid., p. 79; cf. M. Bloch, *La Société féodale*. A later historian of the Annales school has cast doubt on this 'grandfather law', in the case of the seventeenth century at least, on the grounds that grandparents rarely survived long enough to teach their grandchildren: P. Goubert, *The French Peasantry in the Seventeenth Century*, 1982; English translation, Cambridge, 1986. p. 77.

8 I have adopted the phrase 'social memory' from Anna Collard's unpublished paper, given to the ASA conference in 1987, 'Investigating social memory in a Greek context'. Cf. D. Nugent, 'Anthropology, handmaiden of history?', *Critique of Anthropology*, 15 (1985), pp. 71–86.

9 P. Thompson, *The Voice of the Past*, Oxford, 1978, is a good general survey.

10 N. Z. Davis, *Fiction in the Archives*, Stanford, 1987.

11 There is little to note between Bloch's review of Halbwachs, cited above, and the recent studies by P. Nora, 'Mémoire collective' in *La nouvelle histoire*, ed. J. Le Goff, Paris, 1978, and J. Le Goff, 'Memoria' in *Enciclopedia Einaudi*, 8, Turin, 1979, pp. 1068–1109.

12 J. Vansina, *De la tradition orale*, 1961; English translation, London, 1965; revised and retitled *Oral Tradition as History*, Madison, Wisc., 1985.

13 S. Owen, *Remembrances*, Cambridge, Mass., 1986, p. 114. Cf. P. Fussell, *The Great War and Modern Memory*, Oxford, 1975.

14 F. Yates, *The Art of Memory*, London, 1966. Cf. Bartlett, ibid., ch. 11.

15 Good examples are T. Nipperdey, 'Der Kölner Dom als National-denkmal', *Historische Zeitschrift*, 1981, and three essays in P. Nora (ed.), *Les lieux de mémoire*, 1: *La République*, Paris, 1986; Mona

Ozouf on the Panthéon, Maurice Agulhon on the *mairie*, and Antoine Prost on war memorials.

16 W. L. Warner, *The Living and the Dead*, New Haven, Conn., 1959, is a pioneering analysis of Memorial Day by a social anthropologist. Recent studies of rituals of commemoration include C. Amalvi, 'Le 14 Juillet' in *Les lieux de mémoire*, ibid., and S. S. Larsen, 'The Glorious 12th' in *Belonging*, ed. A. P. Cohen, London, 1982.

17 C. Lévi-Strauss, *Tristes tropiques*, Paris, 1955, p. 189.

18 On enclosure in Sweden, see A. Pred, *Place, Practice and Structure*, Cambridge, 1986.

19 A perceptive recent study of the memory of the Indians in colonial Mexico is S. Gruzinski, *La colonisation de l'imaginaire*, Paris, 1988.

20 R. Bastide, 'Mémoire collective et sociologie du bricolage', *Année Sociologique*, 1970, which uses Afro-American religion to criticize and refine the ideas of Halbwachs.

21 F. Bartlett, ibid., pp. 204 f, 299; cf. the central notion of 'Gestalt psychology'. A. Warburg, *Gesammelte Schriften*, 2 vols, Leipzig and Berlin, 1932. E. H. Gombrich, *Art and Illusion*, London, 1960, is a conscious attempt at a synthesis of the Warburg tradition with experimental psychology. A. B. Lord, *The Singer of Tales*, Cambridge, Mass., 1960.

22 P. Fussell, *The Great War and Modern Memory*, Oxford, 1975, pp. 317 f.

23 Ibid., pp. 137 f.

24 W. Y. Tindall, *John Bunyan Mechanick Preacher*, 1934, pp. 22 f.

25 J. Kessler, *Sabbata*, 1540, translated in *Martin Luther*, ed. E. G. Rupp and B. Drewery, London, 1970, pp. 82 f.

26 G. W. Trompf, *The Idea of Historical Recurrence in Western Thought*, Berkeley, 1980.

27 The argument which follows summarizes my articles 'Le roi comme héros populaire', *History of European Ideas*, 3 (1982), pp. 267–71; and 'How to be a Counter-Reformation saint', *Religion and Society in Early Modern Europe*, ed. K. von Greyerz, London, 1984, pp. 45–55.

28 Cf. G. W. Allport, 'The basic psychology of rumour', *Transactions of the American Academy of Sciences* (1945). More speculatively, one might suggest that mechanisms like condensation and displacement, described by Freud in his *Interpretation of Dreams*, are also to be found in these collective dreams or quasi-dreams.

29 Custom was discussed in the article by Bloch cited above. A few medievalists have pursued these questions further: B. Guénée, 'Temps de l'histoire et temps de la mémoire au moyen âge',

1976–7, reprinted in his *Politique et histoire au moyen âge*, Paris, 1981, pp. 253–63; M. Clanchy, *From Memory to Written Record*, London, 1979; Y. Grava, 'La mémoire, une base de l'organization politique des communautés provençales au 14e siècle', in *Temps, mémoire, tradition au moyen âge*. Aix, 1983.

30 I made these points at greater length in 'Through a glass darkly', *History Today*, 35 (November 1985), pp. 6–7. On Irish attitudes to the past, cf. O. Macdonagh, *States of Mind*, London, 1983, chapter 1.

31 J. Barnes, 'The collection of genealogies', *Rhodes-Livingstone Journal*, 5 (1947), p. 52, cited in J. Goody and I. Watt, 'The consequences of literacy', *Comparative Studies in Society and History* (1962–3).

32 E. Hobsbawm and T. Ranger (eds), *The Invention of Tradition*, Cambridge, 1983.

33 E. Weber, *Peasants into Frenchmen*, London, 1976, especially pp. 336 f, on history in schools.

34 For a French example, see J.-C. Martin, *La Vendée et la France*, Paris, 1987, chapter 9, 'La guerre du souvenir'.

35 A case-study exemplifying this approach is C. Wickham, 'Lawyer's time: history and memory in 10th- and 11th-century Italy', in *Studies for R. H. C. Davis*, London, 1985, pp. 53–71.

36 Details in J. Jacquiot, *Médailles et jetons*, Paris, 1968, pp. 617 f.

37 Cf. E. Erikson, 'In search of Gandhi', *Daedalus* (1968), especially pp. 701 f.

38 T. Reik, 'Über kollektives Vergessen', *International Zeitschrift für Psychoanalyse* (1920).

39 Goody and Watt, 'The consequences of literacy', ibid., p. 310.

40 The use of the convenient word 'facts' should not be taken as evidence of a relapse to the positivism criticized earlier. It could be replaced by Thomas Kuhn's favourite term, 'anomalies'.

6

Memory in a Totalitarian Society: The Case of the Soviet Union

Geoffrey A. Hosking

All the fundamental truths about Soviet life are illuminated by oral anecdotes, many of which originate from the mythical Armenian radio. Thus: Armenian radio is asked 'Is it possible to foretell the future?' Answer: 'Yes, that is no problem: we know exactly what the future will be like. Our problem is with the past: that keeps changing.'

This anecdote points up the very distinctive attitude towards time that is officially held in Communist societies. The party leaders are the self-appointed custodians of history. That is the fundamental grounding of their claim to legitimacy. 'Marxism is all-powerful because it is *true*', Lenin used to say. The party has, through its scientific ideology, the key to the objective laws of social evolution, and on that basis exercises the right to administer society.

The party's nationalization of time

This prerogative authority, ostensibly justified by history, underlies what Mikhail Geller calls the party's 'nationalization of time'. In its crudest form this operation was performed in Stalin's *Short Course in the History of the All Union Communist Party (Bolshevik)*, which was the staple diet of all schoolchildren and students in his day. There the October Revolution and the establishment of the Soviet state were seen as the culmination of human evolution, a triumph accomplished essentially by two great men, Lenin, with his disciple Stalin at his side, struggling not only against the bourgeoisie but also against most of their own colleagues who were subsequently unmasked as deviationists, double-dealers or spies. After that victory of good over evil began the era of *planned* time. Lenin inaugurated it with GOELRO, the now virtually forgotten state electrification plan, which he called 'the second party programme', unveiled in 1920. 'Communism equals Soviet power plus electrification of the whole country', he declared. Then Gosplan, the state planning commission, was established in 1921 'to work out a single general state economic plan and the means of implementing it'.

The New Economic Policy, which followed in 1921, was regarded by all party leaders at the time, including Lenin, as a temporary hiccup in this stately progress, for it once again authorized unplanned and unadministered economic transactions on a large scale. Today Gorbachev and his advisers view it differently, and that is a significant fact to which I shall return. But in 1928 this relative anarchy yielded to the first five-year plan. Now this was not an economic plan in the normal sense, as some members of Gosplan protested (only to be arrested as 'wreckers'). That is to say, it was not based on a projection of present productive trends into the future, nor did it attempt to balance one sector of production with another. Rather, especially in its final form, it was the apotheosis of what the economist Naum Jasny has called 'Bacchanalian planning': setting apparently impossible target figures in certain designated key sectors and letting everything else line up behind. 'There are no fortresses which Bolsheviks cannot storm', Stalin exhorted, and furthermore they needed to be stormed, for, as he also remarked at this time, 'We are fifty or a hundred years behind the advanced countries. We must catch up this distance in ten years. Either we do it or we go under.'

The planning of future time was thus raised above the merely empirical and took on at the very outset something of the miraculous – a miracle to be achieved by the ordinary people thanks to the direction of the highest authority, Comrade Stalin. As Katerina Clark has observed in her study of the Soviet novel, this was no ordinary, utilitarian attitude to time. Stimulated by Mircea Eliade's theory of myth, she sees the future projected in the Stalinist vision as a 'Great Time', a transcendent reality in the light of which the phenomena of present-day, profane time acquire their meaning.[1] A five-year plan was a measured stretch of the road leading to paradise.

To the present day the five-year plans have retained something of these sacral qualities. This can be seen in the intricate ritual with which they are elaborated and announced. But most of the effulgent glow has faded. This has been caused partly of course by the now twice-repeated unmasking of Stalin, and partly by the ever more conspicuous divergence between promise and reality. But an important stage in the *Entzauberung* was Khrushchev's attempt in 1961 to set a date (1980) for the achievement of utopia, that is of the creation of the material prerequisites of communism. Not only was this prophecy open to straightforward empirical falsification, but it also confused two categories of time, the profane and the transcendent. (Mind you, the blame for that cannot be put on Khrushchev alone: the confusion is inherent in the Marxist project of creating utopia on earth. Khrushchev merely made it crudely manifest, rushing in, as was his wont, where angels feared to tread.)

As the glow of the Great Future has faded, the party has made some attempt to replace it with a Great Past, for the myth of the lost Golden Age also has a powerful attraction for the human mind, and, moreover, has the advantage that there is no danger of drawing nearer to it and profaning it by finding out what it is really like. Two Great Pasts stand out above all others: the October Revolution and the Great Patriotic War of 1941–5. Both Khrushchev and Gorbachev, as they felt driven to unmask Stalin, have constantly evoked the shade of Lenin as infallible exemplar to guide them in what otherwise might become a kind of moral anarchy. Similarly all Communist leaders of the last generation have claimed a kind of sacral status for present-day Soviet reality on the grounds that it was created by the sacrifice of so many lives in the Second World War. I must emphasize here that I am not denying the reality of those sacrifices, merely trying to elucidate the underlying mythic structures in the official Soviet approach to time.

We can see them conveniently summarized in Gorbachev's speech on the 70th anniversary of the revolution in 1987. He called the anniversary both a 'moment for memory' and a 'look into the future'. Turning to the past, he remembered 'those who forged steel, sowed grain, taught children, advanced science and technology, attained the heights of art', and he evoked 'the solemn memory of those who fell in battle defending their Motherland and who at the cost of their lives gave society the opportunity to advance further.' Looking to the future, he declared that 'Our achievements are immense and highly significant. They are a firm foundation for new accomplishments and for the further development of society. It is in developing socialism, continuing the ideas and practice of Leninism and the October Revolution that we see the meaning of our present-day work and concerns.'[2]

It is not sufficient, however, to examine the myth. For more than a generation now the Soviet Union has been living through a crisis which is inherent in the nature of communist societies. For reasons which I have expounded elsewhere,[3] I suspect that the retrospective dethronement of the Great Leader is an inevitable stage in the evolution of a communist regime. When such *lèse-majesté* is combined with higher standards of education among the population and an increasingly diverse and sophisticated economy, it leads to consequences which render impossible the simple maintenance of the guiding myth. But when the guiding myth is eroded, how much of the authority structure does it bring tumbling down with it? That is the great question to which no one, not even Gorbachev, knows the answer.

This is where the recovery of memory becomes crucial – and by that I mean real memory, not the mythologized substitute. To understand why, one must consider the function of memory in any society, communist or otherwise. Why do schools teach history, institutions accumulate archives, and individuals write memoirs or keep diaries? Surely it is because the life of human beings, both individuals and societies, is not like a game of chess. One cannot look at the present situation and say 'It is irrelevant how we reached this point: the solution to the problem is this.' On the contrary, how we reached this point is crucial. Not only does the route hither contain the habits and tendencies which will continue to affect the onward journey, but it also harbours the missed opportunities, the alternative paths which might have been taken, the embryonic forms which failed to develop into something mature. Reconsidering these features of the landscape helps one both to guard against dangers and to gain a richer awareness of the repertoire of possibilities.

The American political scientist Karl Deutsch put it well when he asserted in his book *The Nerves of Government* that 'memory is essential for any extended functioning of autonomy'.[4] What he meant is that any human institution needs to keep a record of its own activities and to reflect on them from time to time. Rousseau once said that 'Freedom is obedience to the law which we prescribe to ourselves.'[5] As Deutsch explains, 'The "we" in this statement and the whole notion of self-rule implicit in Rousseau's words require memory as an essential element: without it, the self-imposed law could be neither formulated nor remembered.' Nor, I would add, could it be reassessed and if necessary reformulated in the light of experience.

Now of course the Soviet political system is a prime example of an organization which has prescribed a law unto itself. And in a sense it has also maintained elaborate records of its own activity. One can see them, the writings of Lenin, party decrees and enactments, encased in ever more luxurious binding, lining the shelves of every Soviet library. But do they constitute a genuine memory? If they are false or misleading, if the party's conduits of memory are clogged with the rubble of inherited myth, then can the Soviet political system maintain its own autonomy? As Deutsch puts it, 'Without traditions and memory, would-be self-steering organizations are apt to drift with their environment.' Of course, he was envisaging relatively small organizations within a larger society. The Soviet system largely generates its own environment, so that the absence of corrective mechanisms means that damaging tendencies reinforce themselves. Autonomy becomes self-destructive.

I believe that that is what has been happening in the Soviet Union over the last two generations or so. What is much more important, the present Soviet leadership seems to have learnt by bitter experience to recognize the general picture too. As late as a year after coming to power, Gorbachev was still warning members of the Writers' Union, 'If we start probing into the past we shall use up all our energies and come into conflict with the people. We must go forward. We shall deal with the past later.'[6] Not much later, however, he came to the conclusion that 'When we seek the roots of today's difficulties and problems, we do this in order to comprehend their origin and to draw lessons for present-day life from events that go deep into the 1930s.'[7] 'The specific situation in the country [in the 1930s] made us accept forms and methods of socialist construction corresponding to the historical conditions. But those forms were canonized, idealized and turned into dogma. Hence the emasculated image of socialism, the exaggerated centralism in management, the neglect for the rich variety of human life, the pronounced egalitarian tendencies.'[8] We may not feel this analysis goes far enough. But it is undoubtedly a huge step in the right direction.

So the impetus for the resuscitation of real memory is now coming from the very top. But for more than a generation already it has been welling up from below: a constant and growing concern of people in the intellectual and cultural world. Indeed in the face of their long-standing and tenacious pressure, the conversion of the leadership looks belated and half-hearted. To understand where this pressure comes from, we must look at the life experience of the middle and older generation of Soviet citizens of today.

Collectivization and the suppression of memory

Perhaps I am wrong, but it has always seemed to me that there is one particular event which, above all, motivated the distortion and suppression of historical truth. That was the mass collectivization of agriculture of 1929–30, and the attendant process of so-called 'dekulakization'. For this was when the interests of the emergent ruling class of town and countryside most brutally and destructively overrode not just the interests but the very way of life and economy of the great majority of ordinary Soviet people. Most Western scholars would, I think, now agree that the collectivization was carried through in order to end the relative autonomy (economic, but therefore also political) enjoyed by millions of private peasant households, and to subject them to the direct rule of the emergent party-state apparatus. There were subsidiary considerations as well, such as the grain shortage of 1928–9, which acted as an immediate precipitant, but there were many other possible solutions to that problem: the one the party leadership chose was the one which accorded with its fundamental interests as a not yet very secure ruling class.

The result was to tear the heart from the village community. The envy and greed of its poorest, least established members were deliberately whipped up and directed against the pillars of rural society. The wealthiest, or the most resistant, were altogether expropriated and deported from the village. The rest were put under overwhelming pressure to join the new collective farms and to surrender their property to them – in some cases *all* their property. Only gradually was a compromise reached, by which households were able to retain their own houses and garden plots, together with the animals and tools required to cultivate the latter. The destructive frenzy caused by this 'turning upside down' of the traditional rural community is by now better documented – at least in the West – than it used to be. Peasants sold up and moved out if they could; they slaughtered and ate their cattle; some even burnt down their houses, determined that they should not fall into the hands of the 'anti-Christ'. The long-term effects were even more disastrous: the demoralization and loss of autonomy suffered by the village community were such that, from then on, its younger and more talented or ambitious members would do their utmost to escape from it. Even the notorious passport restrictions could not prevent the young men from flooding into the towns in droves to seek a somewhat more independent existence there (young women found it more difficult). 'Stadtluft macht frei' became in effect the slogan of two or three generations of rural youth. The collective farms had to be run by women and old people. The legacy of underproductive agriculture became a permanent feature of Soviet life, and remains so to the present day.

Pasternak surmised in *Doctor Zhivago* that collectivization was such a hideous mistake that it had to be concealed at all costs, 'and so it was necessary by intimidation to break people from the habit of thinking and making judgements, to compel them to see the non-existent, and to argue the opposite of what was obvious to everyone. Hence the unprecedented savagery of the Ezhovshchina, the proclamation of a constitution not intended for application, and the introduction of elections not based on the elective principle.'[9] The habit of 'doublethink', already perceptible, became hardened and durable. A split opened up inside each individual between what one knew and what one was allowed to say – a split made more complicated by the powerful effects of self-deception. It was after all only too tempting for members of the new elite to believe what they were told, even against strong evidence. As Raisa Orlova, then a student at Moscow University, admits in her memoirs: 'I passionately wanted to be happy, and lived with my eyes tightly closed. . . . Everything negative in our life simply bounced off us, extruded by our whole frame of mind.'[10] Many served the Stalinist state out of profound devotion, sometimes but by no means always bolstered by self-interest.

The forms assumed by this inner split were manifold. But for many people it manifested itself in what one might call a spiritual schism between the urban and the rural. After all, during the next generation for millions of Soviet citizens the decisive life experience was the migration from village to town, usually at quite a young age, to serve in the army or to gain secondary or higher education, having completed which they would not return home, but would move heaven and earth to find urban employment and living space – often enduring years, even a lifetime, in crowded and sub-standard accommodation in order to do so. In a sense, their years of individual dedication to the urban ideal replicated the total historical experience of the Soviet state, with its dedication to industry, technology, education, culture and the mass media. Both in the macrocosm and the microcosm, this dedication was achieved at the cost, not only of turning one's back on a rural childhood, but also of denigrating it, devaluing it, as something to flee from at all costs. How many Soviet citizens have, in this way, denied their own childhoods?

The rescue of memory

It is symptomatic, then, that in Soviet culture the rescue of memory began with the rediscovery of rural childhood. In the short-lived independent literary almanac *Literaturnaya Moskva* in 1956 an otherwise unknown writer, Nikolai Zhdanov, told of a secure and well-established party official returning to his native village for the funeral of his mother, whom he has not seen for many years. He rediscovers in the crosses of the cemetery, in the smell of incense, in the crude wooden furniture of his former home, a world which 'according to his conceptions had long ceased to exist'. It all becomes too much for him and to escape painful memories, as well as the pleas of villagers who have a rare opportunity to bend the ear of a high official, he cuts his visit short and hastens back to his comfortable carpeted office in town. But even safely re-ensconced there, he cannot shake off his impressions, and the timid question of a peasant woman he encountered: 'Have they done right by us or not?'[11]

This story was much noticed and commented upon. It was the first harbinger of a trend which later included Solzhenitsyn's *Matryona's Home* in 1963, and then from the mid-1960s a stream of novels and stories dealing with rural life. This so-called 'village prose' has a complicated relationship with the official myth. In some respects it seems a direct denial of it. Thus village writers usually emphasize the backwardness and traditionalism of the way of life they are describing, almost as if to mock the great project of modernization. Again the outlook of the characters, and usually of the narrator as well, is deliberately limited in its horizons, divorced from any intellectual system or broader understanding of history, as if self-sufficient and self-validating: there is no trace of *ideinost'* (ideological consciousness) or *partiinost'* (party-mindedness).

All the same, as one gets used to the genre, a question suggests itself. Is not the rejection of the official myth so wilful that we are perhaps dealing here with a kind of mirror image of it? We have seen that the officially projected Great Future has a tendency to yield to a Great Past, or Golden Age. Is 'village prose' perhaps an alternative version of this Golden Age, but more powerful and convincing because it incorporates features so long displaced from consciousness. Sidney Monas, following Bakhtin, has written of the great potency manifested by the 'return of the repressed' in a culture bounded by censorship.[12] 'Village prose' contains many previously repressed elements: it resurrects the ideal of the peasant community, long espoused by the populists and their heirs, but despised by the Communists and destroyed to make way for the collective farm, which was based on entirely different, authoritarian principles. At first timidly, but then with increasing conviction, the village writers have approached the challenge of writing a true history of the collectivization of agriculture, a task which their historian colleagues have so far funked. Perhaps most important of all, the village writers have revived ideals of gentleness, kindness, acceptance of human failings which are derived from the Christian tradition, and are diametrically opposed to the Communist virtues of constant activity, struggle and merciless rejection of the backward and fallible.

How was it possible to publish such material in a cultural milieu so tightly controlled by the political authorities? This is a subject I have dealt with elsewhere,[13] but briefly: I would say that in a totalitarian society it is inevitable that 'mutual protection groups' or 'family circles' will arise, to provide a degree of shelter from the overwhelming demands of the state. When mass terror is no longer applied, these circles proliferate, flourish and provide not only protection but often a modicum of comfort, even prosperity for their members. In the cultural world, such circles, in the form of individual journals, theatres, cinema studios, and so on, have the potential to go even further and act as islands of non-conformity. This is, in my view, the first stage in the creation of civil society, and it is no accident that its first project is the recovery of memory. Thus *Novy mir* under Tvardovskii acted as the forum for the first publication of village prose, but after his downfall other journals, notably *Nash sovremennik*, under his enemy, Sergei Vikulov, proved capable of continuing the tradition. This should not surprise us: 'family circles' are often as hostile to one another as they are to the political forces from which they seek security. The anomaly at any rate proves that the tradition had become a powerful one, not to be obstructed simply because one home had been closed to it.

But the drive for the recovery of memory has manifested itself not only in literary journals and not only in the search for lost rural community. Starting in the mid-1960s and with gathering force since then, individuals and groups, official and unofficial, have been concerning themselves with the rescue or revival of the inheritance of the past. The greatest literary monument to this concern is of course Alexander Solzhenitsyn's *The Gulag Archipelago*, compiled from the testimony, written and oral, of 227 individuals and dedicated by the author as a 'collective memorial to all those who were tortured and killed'.[14]

A similar aspiration moved the anonymous group of editors who in 1976 began to compile an unofficial journal called *Pamyat'* (Memory), consisting of memoirs, diaries, letters and other documents bearing witness to those aspects of the past not admissible in official Soviet publications. The editorial introduction declared: 'There is a grave illness known as amnesia. It condemns the individual to loss of the most important and valuable human characteristics, the sense of continuity and of being linked with one's own past. What then are the consequences if such an illness, for historical or other reasons, should affect society as a whole?'[15]

Preserving the national heritage and the natural environment

Evidence of much broader, indeed mass support for the revival of the nation's historical memory is provided by the formation and spectacular growth of the All-Russian Society for the Preservation of Cultural and Historical Monuments. It was set up in 1966 after a campaign by writers such as Vladimir Soloukhin. The impetus for its establishment was given by (1) Khrushchev's campaign of closing and destroying numerous churches between 1959 and 1964; (2) the extensive rebuilding of Soviet cities, especially Moscow, which entailed the bulldozing of ancient buildings, gardens and squares.

After about a decade, VOOPIK (to give it its Russian

acronym) had reached a reported membership of twelve million. Yet the society never acquired its own journal (probably a sign of political reservations about its existence, though there were always high officials on its administrative board). However, it maintained good relations with some established journals, like *Molodaya gvardiya* and *Nash sovremennik*, both of which identified with the Russian national tendency. It has raised funds and volunteers to carry out restoration projects, such as the monastery of St Kirill at Beloozero and the New Jerusalem monastery at Istra outside Moscow. It has sponsored tourism in Russia's old towns and has collected information to use in a campaign against the closure of so-called 'villages without a future' (*besperspektivnye derevni*) in the non-Black-Earth region. Altogether, although the aims of VOOPIK are still far from being fully realized, there can be no doubting the society's achievement in mobilizing public concern about problems which were previously scarcely acknowledged by the authorities.[16]

Public concern about preservation extends not only to buildings, but also to the natural environment. Over the last generation or so, evidence has mounted of ceaseless environmental degradation under pressure from industrial development, and some of this evidence has found its way into the press and been seriously debated. This is remarkable in a country where for so long, as I have pointed out, industrial development had assumed a sacred role. Blast furnaces, power stations and chemical plants were constructed at great speed and left to spread their fumes over the air, and to discharge their effluents into the rivers. Hydro-electric power stations like Dneproges, one of the showpieces of the first five-year plan, have flooded thousands of acres of agricultural land and forest, while beneath them rivers have become shallow or even dried up. Even agricultural improvement projects can have damaging results, if poorly executed: thus the marshy Poles'e area of Belorussia was so ineptly drained that in certain areas sand dunes formed and even dust storms developed. As local wisecracks commented, aping the propaganda machine, 'In the next five-year plan let us transform all the marshes of Belorussia into deserts!'[17]

The first major public environmental campaign was mounted a

generation ago to defend Lake Baikal. In the late 1950s there was a project to build a cellulose factory on its banks, to manufacture a tough variety of cord, probably for bomber aircraft. The project required especially pure water, which is why Baikal was chosen as the location.

Protest against the project began in 1961. What was unusual about this protest was that it originated not from rival ministries competing for investment funds, but from scientists and writers motivated by altruistic concern about the environment. As far as I know, it was the first major articulation of such concern in the Soviet Union. Probably it is explained by (1) Baikal's unique status as the world's largest reservoir of fresh water; (2) the fact that Khrushchev's anti-Stalin campaign had reached its height, which seemed to legitimate protest against authoritarian government; and (3) evidence was beginning to accumulate of the serious environmental damage which had been caused by previous major industrial projects. On and off, the campaign to save Baikal has continued over the whole of the intervening quarter century. It has not saved Baikal from serious pollution, but has perhaps alleviated its extent. It certainly caused serious delays in the completion of the cellulose factory, and compelled it to adopt filtering methods more thorough than any previously applied in the Soviet Union.[18]

In some ways an even more remarkable public campaign was that undertaken against the project to divert some of the north-flowing rivers of European Russia and Siberia to irrigate the semi-arid regions of Central Asia, Kazakhstan and the Volga basin. Schemes of this kind had been discussed ever since the 1930s, and attained especial urgency during the 1970s because of a disastrous fall in the level of the Aral Sea. Economists blanched at the huge costs involved, but nevertheless at the 25th party congress in 1976 full-scale scientific studies of the project were commissioned, and in 1981 at the 26th congress preliminary construction work was authorized.[19]

From the start the project had the powerful backing of Gosplan and of the Ministry of Water Resources and Melioration, both of which stood to gain in prestige, funding and staff from it. The same applied to the party organizations of the Asian republics, who tend normally to feel themselves at a disadvantage compared with the Slavs. Opposition, as in the case of Baikal, took much longer to mobilize. But gradually the disquiet of the economists was reinforced by that of the soil scientists, worried about salination and erosion, and then, most effectively of all, by conservationists, concerned that the river diversion would lead to flooding and to the submersion of some of Russia's most valuable historical monuments, the churches and monasteries of the north, most of which lie along river banks and are vulnerable to any rise in the water level.

This theme was taken up in the summer of 1986 at the 8th Writers' Union Congress, which turned into the most concerted public demonstration yet seen of concern at the joint destruction of the natural environment and the historical past. The mood was summed up by the poet Andrei Voznesenskii who, after attacking the rivers project, uttered a general warning. 'Our culture has been so over-exploited that it is drying up like the rivers! I am talking here about what worries me most, the threat of spiritual emptiness, about the ecology of culture. Our indifference destroys the past, as it has already destroyed the Sukharev tower. Our indifference distorts the present – consider how impersonal and indistinguishable today are Moscow, Tbilisi and Tashkent! And what is worst of all, we are destroying the future.'[20] Shortly after the Writers' Congress the Politburo ordered all construction work on the rivers project to be stopped. This was not necessarily the final defeat for it, but it was certainly a very severe setback, incomparably greater than the Baikal scheme had ever suffered.

Most writers agreed about the 'ecology of culture'. This agreement does not generate harmony, however, for the Soviet Union is a multi-national society, and each nation wants to rescue its own heritage from the 'impersonal and indistinguishable' which so oppresses Voznesenskii. Solzhenitsyn in his Nobel speech praised literature's capacity for conveying a national tradition and warned of the consequences for a nation of disrupting that tradition. 'Such a nation does not remember itself, it is deprived of its spiritual unity, and although its population supposedly have a common language, fellow-countrymen suddenly stop understanding each other.'[21] This was a leitmotif of the speeches at the 1986 Writers' Congress, and was expressed with particular vigour by the non-Russians, who feel themselves threatened by increased use of the Russian language, accompanied by the reduction of their own to a kind of domestic and farmyard status. As the Armenian poet Silva Kaputikyan complained in an article in *Pravda*, 'We in Armenia find that the scope for using one's native language contracts year by year. Not only in all-Soviet institutions but also in purely local ones Armenian is gradually ceasing to be used for every-day business. This has created a situation where parents are sometimes reluctant to send their children to Armenian schools. It's obvious why: when a language is used mainly in private life, it loses its age-old capacity to participate in the general progress of human thought.'[22] Thus one man's memory may be another's creeping oblivion.

Some Russians who feel themselves similarly threatened by the 'impersonal and indistinguishable' have a tendency to seek a national explanation too, and, having no larger neighbour on whom they can vent their frustration, turn instead on the Jews. This is a tendency we have seen all too clearly recently in the unofficial society which ironically calls itself *Pamyat'* (Memory).

So we must not imagine that the recovery of memory is a smooth and harmonious process. On the contrary, its paths are diverse and contradictory, and are bound to generate strife. But what we are witnessing today is the painful return of a society from totalitarian rigidity to a kind of normality. There is still a long way to go, and much conflict is inherent in the process, but I think it can already be said that the recovery of memory was a decisive stage, without which further progress would be imposs-ible. A society without a (tolerably authentic) knowledge of its past is strongly handicapped in its dealing with the future. Deprived of a self-correcting mechanism, it will thrash around blindly, compounding mistakes or exaggeratedly overcorrecting them, rather as Khrushchev did a generation ago, not least because his disclosure of the past was so partial and selective. I think we can sense in the Soviet media today a greater sobriety and a closer contact with reality than at any time perhaps since the early 1930s. This is not a sufficient condition for the creation of a freer society, but it is certainly a necessary one.

Notes

1 K. Clarke, *The Soviet Novel: History as Ritual*, University of Chicago Press, 1981, pp. 39–40.
2 *Literaturnaya gazeta*, 4 Nov. 1987, p. 1.
3 G. Hosking, *A History of the Soviet Union*, London: Fontana, 1985, chapter 12.
4 K. Deutsch, *The Nerves of Government*, New York: Free Press of Glencoe, 1963, p. 206.
5 J. J. Rousseau, *The Social Contract*, book 1, chapter 8.
6 Radio Svoboda: *Issledovatel'skii byulleten'*, 113 (1986), p. 2.
7 M. Gorbachev, *Perestroika: New Thinking for our Country and the World*, London: Collins, 1987, p. 43.
8 Ibid., p. 45.
9 B. Pasternak, *Doctor Zhivago*, Milan: Feltrinelli, 1957, p. 519.
10 R. Orlova, *Vospominaniya o neproshedshem vremeni: Moskva 1961–1981 gg.*, Ann Arbor, Mich.: Ardis, 1983.
11 N. Zhdanov, 'Poezdka na rodinu', *Literaturnaya Moskva*, 2 (1956), pp. 404–15.
12 S. Monas, 'Censorship as a way of life', in G. Hosking and G. Cushing (eds), *Perspectives on Literature in Eastern and Western Europe*, London: Macmillan (forthcoming).
13 G. Hosking, 'The Institutionalisation of Soviet Literature', in Hosking and Cushing, ibid.
14 A. Solzhenitsyn, *The Gulag Archipelago*, vol. 1, p. 10.
15 *Pamyat'*, 1, Moscow, 1976, New York: Khronika Press, 1978, p. v.
16 J. Dunlop, *The Faces of Contemporary Russian Nationalism*, Princeton University Press, 1983, chapter 3.
17 B. Komarov, *Unichtozhenie prirody*, Frankfurt am Main: Posev, 1978, p. 73.
18 M. Goldman, *The Spoils of Progress: Environmental Pollution in the Soviet Union*, Cambridge, Mass.: MIT Press, 1972, chapter 6; *Izvestiya*, 7 Oct. 1987.
19 *Russkaya mysl'*, 15 July 1982, p. 11.
20 *Literaturnaya gazeta*, 2 July 1986, p. 6.
21 A. Solzhenitsyn, 'One Word of Truth . . .: the Nobel Speech', London: Bodley Head, 1970, p. 16.
22 S. Kaputikyan, *Pravda*, 7 May 1987.

7

Forms of Memory and Memory of Forms in English Poetry

Jon Stallworthy

The ancient Greeks knew Mnemosyne to be the mother of the Muses, Poetry to be the daughter of Memory, and a poet – Simonides of Ceos – is credited with the invention of the *art* of memory.[1]

In honour of the Greek connection, I begin in Greece – not ancient Greece, but Modern Greece struggling to be born – where, in what was to be his last journal, Lord Byron wrote the poem 'On This Day I Complete My Thirty-Sixth Year', which opens:

> 'Tis time this heart should be unmoved
> Since others it hath ceased to move:
> Yet, though I cannot be beloved,
> Still let me love!

He has in mind one particular 'other' – his Greek page boy Loucas – who re-minded him perhaps of the Cambridge choirboy, John Edleston, some of whose hair he still carried in a locket. Edleston had returned his love, as Loucas did not. A later stanza of the poem tells us that Byron has others in mind, as he exhorts himself to

> Think through *whom*
> Thy life-blood tracks its parent lake,
> And then strike home!

He remembers the martial ancestors celebrated in one of his earliest poems, 'On Leaving Newstead Abbey', and his metaphor of the parent lake suggests a subliminal recollection of *Newstead* Lake. Twenty years before, he had taken his leave of the Abbey with its tombs of crusader Byrons in these terms:

> Shades of heroes, farewell! your descendant, departing
>   From the seat of his ancestors, bids you, adieu!
> Abroad, or at home, your remembrance imparting
>   New courage, he'll think upon glory, and you.

Now, at the end of a lifetime's quest for a cause worth fighting for, he returns to chivalric concepts and chivalric diction: the hero, shield and field, glory and grave. So much for the memory of the lover and the soldier on 22 January 1824. What of the memory of the poet?

> My days are in the yellow leaf;
>   The flowers and fruits of love are gone;
> The worm, the canker, and the grief
>   Are mine alone!

That melancholy music so expressive of his theme – the closing dimeter ('Are mine alone!') that, failing to fulfil the expectations of a tetrameter, prepares the listener for unfulfilment, premature death – we have heard before; *he* had heard before.

> O what can ail thee, Knight at arms,
>   Alone and palely loitering?
> The sedge has withered from the lake
>   And no birds sing.

Byron told John Murray he 'did not approve of Keats's poetry, or principles of poetry', and his biographer, Leslie Marchand, says that it seems 'he cast [*Lamia, Isabella, The Eve of St. Agnes, and Other Poems*] aside without reading it.' It does not seem so to me. It seems, rather, that we have a classic example of a singer's subliminal memory of a song, a poet's memory of a tune, the sound of a specific stanza. And was Keats the composer of that tune? I believe not. I believe he was prompted by a subliminal memory of George Herbert's poem 'Virtue', which begins:

Sweet day, so cool, so calm, so bright,
The bridal of the earth and sky:
The dew shall weep thy fall tonight;
    For thou must die.

Sweet rose, whose hue angry and brave
Bids the rash gazer wipe his eye:
Thy root is ever in its grave,
    And thou must die.

Once again the cadence of the earlier poem smuggles its substance into the later. The Knight at arms 'must die', and Keats's kaleidoscopic memory reorders the elements of Herbert's poem: *sweet, day, dew, weep, rose, eye, root*. Was Herbert, then, the composer of that tune? Perhaps in its English form, but Mr Julian Roberts has suggested that he may have been influenced in his choice of the short line by that of the characteristic Horatian stanza:

Persicos odi, puer, apparatus,
displicent nexae philyra coronae;
mitte sectari, rosa quo locorum
    sera moretur.

My argument is for a form of poetic influence related to that proposed by Harold Bloom, but significantly different from it. In a series of books, starting with *The Anxiety of Influence*,[2] he advanced a theory of influence based on what Freud calls 'the family romance': the child's desire to supplant its parent, 'to be the father of himself'. Poetic influence, says Bloom,

> when it involves two strong, authentic poets, always proceeds by a misreading of the prior poet, an act of creative correction that is actually and necessarily a misinterpretation. The history of fruitful poetic influence, which is to say the main tradition of Western poetry since the Renaissance, is a history of anxiety and self-saving caricature, of distortion, of perverse, wilful revisionism without which modern poetry as such could not exist.[3]

Bloom is concerned with one poet's essentially Oedipal engage-
ment with a predecessor: Wordsworth's with Milton, Browning's
with Shelley. Whatever one may think of his theoretical
framework, many of his illustrations of the poet's memory at
work are subtle and persuasive. His arguments, however, take
virtually no account of the formal relationship between poems,
and this is one of the things that interests me in Byron's
dreamlike transformation of Keats's 'La Belle Dame'. How are
we to account for this mysterious phenomenon? Byron can
hardly be accused of Oedipal urges towards a younger poet.

I suggest that, as the latter-day Crusader brooded on un-
requited love among the swamps of Missolonghi, his subconscious perceived a similarity between his plight and that of
the Knight at arms; a perception summoning to his inner ear a
distant echo of Keats's lament. From there, it entered his
consciousness not as an echo of the old but an annunciation of
the new. Meanwhile his *sub*-conscious, at its dreamwork of re-
creation, was developing a detail of Keats's poem into one half of
a structural antithesis. La Belle Dame's lover is a Knight at arms,
but his profession is not of central importance to the poem,
whereas Byron perceives a bitter opposition between the roles of
lover and warrior. He had long been regarded – and, indeed,
regarded himself – as a paradoxical, antithetical figure. In 1814,
he had told his fiancée of a visit from the German phrenologist
Johann Spurzheim:

> He says all [my faculties and dispositions] are strongly marked –
> but very antithetical for every thing developed in & on this same
> skull of mine has its *opposite* in great force so that to believe him
> my good & evil are at perpetual war . . . .

The metaphor of 'perpetual war' is appropriate, in that no
antithesis is more central to Byron's life and poetry than that of
love and war: 'fierce loves and faithless wars' as he put it in *Don
Juan*, mischievously misquoting Spenser's 'fierce wars and
faithless loves'.

Setting out to mark the completion of his thirty-sixth year, he
gives precedence to love, reversing the sequence of Keats's

poem. But as he finds words to fit his emerging tune, images of autumnal landscape and anguished lover –

> My days are in the yellow leaf;
> The flowers and fruits of love are gone . . .

overlap as in the earlier poem:

> The sedge has withered from the lake . . . .
> And on thy cheeks a fading rose
> Fast withereth too.

Byron's dissonant rhyme, 'gone'/'alone', echoes Keats's use of 'alone' and *his* dissonant rhyme, 'woebegone'/'done'. The circular garland, bracelets and girdle (perhaps of daisy-chain), that the Knight had made the Lady, now reappear dream-transformed into a prisoner's chain and the circular wreath that 'decks the hero's bier,/Or binds his brow' – surely the lily-white brow of Keats's hero.

At the climax of the Knight at arms' tale, his memory of love is succeeded by a dream of death, a vision of Kings, Princes, and warriors all as death-pale as he was himself to become:

> I saw their starved lips in the gloam
> With horrid warning gapéd wide,
> And I awoke, and found me here
> On the cold hill's side.

With that awakening, Keats's ballad returns to its bleak beginning. Byron's memories of love are similarly interrupted – 'Awake, my spirit!' – and succeeded by a premonition of death on a 'Field' as desolate as the Knight at arms' 'cold hill's side'.

Keats is one of the most musical and memorable of English poets and his influence can be seen and heard in the work of many of his successors. Bloom speaks of 'the embarrassment of reading *The Scholar-Gipsy* and *Thyrsis*, and finding the odes of Keats crowding out poor Arnold'. I do not share his embarrassment and, in my own reading of 'The Scholar-Gipsy', do not find Keats crowding out its author any more than he crowded out the author of 'On This Day I Complete My Thirty-Sixth Year'. These poems seem to me examples of the same creative phenomenon.

The story of the Scholar-Gipsy – who two hundred years before had preferred life among the hedgerows to a more conventional career – touched Arnold deeply. It brought into focus his dissatisfaction with his own life in an urban present, his nostalgia for a rural past associated (he told his brother) with 'that life at Oxford, the *freest* and most delightful part, perhaps of my life, when with you and Clough and Walrond I shook off all the bonds and formalities of the place, and enjoyed the spring of life and that unforgotten Oxfordshire and Berkshire country'. Brooding on the bleak contrast between here and now, there and then, I believe he subconsciously perceived a similarity between his situation and that of Keats contemplating a nightingale, which had never known

> The weariness, the fever, and the fret
> Here, where men sit and hear each other groan . . . .

Again I suspect an echo apprehended as annunciation; one that, as Arnold began to feel his way into his poem, guided him in his choice of a ten-line stanza differing from that of Keats's Ode only in its rhyme-scheme and the positioning of its one short line. The eighth line of Keats's stanza differs from the rest in that it has three feet rather than five. Arnold similarly varies his pentameters with a trimeter, but, by making it the sixth of his ten lines, he effectively divides his stanza into two unequal parts. This off-centre division of the stanza is repeated in the larger structure of the poem as a whole. Thirteen stanzas about the pastoral past are followed by twelve about the tormented present in much the same way that contrary states are juxtaposed in individual stanzas: day and night in the first, here and there in the second.

At the end of Keats's Ode, the speaker, who has been transported by the nightingale 'on the viewless wings of Poesy', asks 'Was it a vision, or a waking dream?' Arnold's transformation of that vision or that waking dream emerges in the second part of his poem. The search for the Scholar-Gipsy, which had occupied the first part, is brutally interrupted at line 131:

> But what – I dream! Two hundred years are flown
> Since first thy story ran through Oxford halls . . . .

But no sooner does he admit that the object of his quest must long since have found an unknown grave than he challenges that admission:

> The generations of thy peers are fled,
> And we ourselves shall go;
> But how possessest an immortal lot . . . .

He addresses the Scholar-Gipsy as Keats had addressed the nightingale:

> Thou wast not born for death, immortal Bird!
> No hungry generations tread thee down . . . .

The immortal Bird has undergone a dream-transformation into an immortal Gipsy. Keats, intoxicated by the nightingale's song, had longed to

> leave the world unseen,
> And with thee fade away into the forest dim:
> Fade far away, dissolve, and quite forget
> What thou among the leaves hast never known,
> The weariness, the fever, and the fret
> Here, where men sit and hear each other groan;
> Where palsy shakes a few, sad, last grey hairs,
> Where youth grows pale, and spectre-thin, and dies . . . .

The Scholar-Gipsy 'early didst . . . leave the world' – Keats's very phrase –

> Before this strange disease of modern life,
> With its sick hurry, its divided aims,
> Its head o'ertaxed, its palsied hearts, was rife . . . .

But whereas the listener in Keats's ode had exclaimed 'Away! away! for I will fly to thee', Arnold's Gipsy is urged to 'fly our paths, our feverish contact fly!' lest

> then thy glad perennial youth would fade,
> Fade, and grow old at last, and die like ours.

The unseen nightingale had been imagined singing to 'the Queen-Moon', although where the listener stood there was

> no light
> Save what from heaven is with the breezes blown . . . .

So in Arnold's poem, the Gipsy is twice glimpsed by moonlight and is said to have spent his life in the quest for a secret, 'waiting for the spark from heaven to fall'. He flies from his pursuing poet – as the nightingale from his – and is last seen revealing his secret store of knowledge in an image with a Keatsian origin. The nightingale had

> Charmed magic casements, opening on the foam
> Of perilous seas,

and it is through such seas, 'through sheets of foam', that Arnold's Tyrian trader sails to find the beach where he will undo his corded bales.

There are other Keatsian echoes and images in 'The Scholar-Gipsy' – the most significant being the nightingales of line 220 – but, taken together, they seem to me no cause for embarrassment. Rather, I see them as essential parts of a new poetic structure, a beautiful variation on a Keatsian theme.

My third example of a poet's transformation of a text held in the depths of memory does not signal the fact with a shared stanza-form, but the line-length is the same and the cadence unmistakable:

> That is no country for old men. The young
> In one another's arms, birds in the trees
> – Those dying generations – at their song . . . .

'No hungry generations tread thee down'. Yeats's 'Sailing to Byzantium' offers another variation of Keats's 'Ode to a Nightingale', another escape from mortality and mutability into 'the artifice of eternity'.

That country, which the old poet acknowledges is not for him, is Keats's 'country green'; those 'birds in the trees', that

> commend all summer long
> Whatever is begotten, born and dies,

are clearly descended from the 'Dryad of the trees' that 'Singest of summer in full-throated ease'. And as Keats had longed to

> leave the world unseen
> And with thee fade away into the forest dim . . .

so Yeats makes his decision to move on:

> And therefore I have sailed the seas and come
> To the holy city of Byzantium.

His heart is 'sick with desire' – as Keats's heart aches – and where the precursor had sought to join the 'immortal Bird' 'on the viewless wings of Poesy', Yeats carries the identification further. He *becomes* the bird, one that keeps 'a drowsy Emperor awake' by singing 'of what is past, or passing, or to come'. Other emperors had heard a similar song. Keats's speaker had said:

> The voice I hear this passing night was heard
> In ancient days by emperor and clown . . . .

'Byzantium' is closely related to 'Sailing to Byzantium'. Yeats wrote to his friend Sturge Moore:

The poem originates from a criticism of yours. You objected to the last verse of 'Sailing to Byzantium' because a bird made by a goldsmith was just as natural as anything else. That showed me that the idea needed exposition.

'Byzantium' is again a transformation of the 'Ode to a Nightingale'; drawing its 'path', 'midnight', 'Emperor', from the earlier poem, together with the bird that, singing between moon and star, recalls another song, another night:

> Already with thee! tender is the night,
>   And haply the Queen-Moon is on her throne,
>   Clustered around by all her starry Fays . . . .

Keats's vision is put to flight by a word – 'Forlorn!' – a word repeated,

>   like a bell
> To toll me back from thee to my sole self!

Yeats's vision ends on a similar note, with the 'great cathedral gong' of the first stanza reverberating over 'That dolphin-torn, that gong-tormented sea'.

If further evidence were needed of the process of transformation I am describing, it is to be found where one might expect to find it: in the manuscript drafts of both 'Sailing to Byzantium' and 'Byzantium'. Before Yeats's speaker 'sailed the seas' to Byzantium, he declared:

> I fly from nature to Byzantium
> Among these sun browned pleasant mariners . . . .

The flight is unmistakable, as also, I think, is the echo of Keats's 'sunburnt mirth'; and the drafts of both Byzantium poems have the 'gong-tormented sea' flecked with Keatsian 'foam'.

To my mind, there can be no doubt that Byron, Arnold, and Yeats have each produced a transformation of a Keatsian poem, but can one be so sure that at the time of composition they were unaware of the fact? Perhaps not, but Bloom argues for – and an experience of my own would seem to confirm – the existence of a repressive censoring mechanism that makes the poet's conscious mind forget what the subconscious so fruitfully remembers.

In writing a poem called 'The Almond Tree', I had the poet-father of a new-born son say:

> Welcome
> to your white sheet
> my best poem!

I will not deny that I was stunned when a friend spoke of 'the nod to Ben Jonson', and went on to quote the lines from Jonson's elegy 'On my First Son':

> 'Here doth lie
> Ben Jonson his best piece of poetry.'

I would have been prepared to swear in a court of law that I had never read or heard that poem, but obviously I had. If my theft – or, as I now prefer to call it, my transformation – had been pointed out to me while I was still writing 'The Almond Tree', I am sure I would have cursed and cancelled those lines, not perceiving the best thing about them: the fact that, while Jonson's lines about a dead son are echoed in a happy context, they anticipate my speaker's subsequent *un*happy discovery that his son is a Down's Syndrome or mongol child. In the same way (if I may liken great things to small), I believe – though clearly I cannot prove – that if Byron, Arnold and Yeats had in the act of writing their poems become aware of the debt to Keats, they would either have lost the confidence necessary to complete them, or at the very least have gone to greater lengths to hide their loot.

I am supported here (or, if I am honest, I should say that Harold Bloom and I are both anticipated) by T. S. Eliot who, in July 1919, wrote in *The Egoist*:

> There is a kind of stimulus for a writer which is more important than the stimulus of admiring another writer. Admiration leads most often to imitation, we can seldom remain long unconscious of our imitating another, and the awareness of our debt naturally leads us to hatred of the object imitated.

Eliot goes on to speak of a stimulus to creation undreamt of in Bloom's philosophy:

> If we stand toward a writer in this other relation of which I speak we do not imitate him, and though we are quite as likely to be accused of it, we are quite unperturbed by the charge. This relation is a feeling of profound kinship, or rather of a peculiar personal intimacy, with another, probably a dead author. It may overcome us suddenly, on first or after long acquaintance; it is certainly a crisis; and when a young person is seized with his first passion of this sort he may be changed, metamorphosed almost, within a few weeks even, from a bundle of second-hand sentiments into a person. The imperative intimacy arouses for the first time a real, an unshakable confidence. That you possess this secret knowledge, this intimacy, with the dead man, that after few or many years or centuries you should have appeared, with this indubitable claim to distinction; who can penetrate at once the thick and dusty circumlocutions about his reputation, can call yourself alone his friend: it is something more than *encouragement* to you. It is a cause of development, like personal relations in life. Like personal intimacies in life, it may and probably will pass, but it will be ineffaceable.

Christopher Ricks is surely right to see the Dantesque section of Eliot's *Little Gidding* as an example of just such intimacy with a dead author.[4] Eliot, the fire-watcher in the London Blitz, remembers – and wants us, his readers, to remember – his predecessor's experience of a greater Inferno:

> In the uncertain hour before the morning
> Near the ending of interminable night
> At the recurrent end of the unending . . . .

The indentation of the lines alerts the eye, as the hint of a rhyme ('morning'/'unending') alerts the ear, to the presence of a ghostly *terza rima*, the verse form of Dante's *Divine Comedy*. Elevated diction and elaborate syntax confirm those signals:

> And as I fixed upon the down-turned face
> That pointed scrutiny with which we challenge

The first-met stranger in the waning dusk
I caught the sudden look of some dead master
Whom I had known, forgotten, half recalled
Both one and many; in the brown baked features
The eyes of a familiar compound ghost
Both intimate and unidentifiable.

Repetition being of the nature of Hell, it seems quite natural that this meeting with a dead master should mirror, should echo, that of Eliot's predecessor with *his* dead master, Brunetto Latini. In Canto XV, Dante tells us:

> we met a troop of spirits, who were coming
> alongside the bank; and each looked at us,
> as in the evening men are wont
>
> to look at one another under a new moon; and
> towards us sharpened their vision, as an aged
> tailor does at the eye of a needle.
>
> Thus eyed by that family, I was recognized by
> one who took me by the skirt, and said:
> 'What a wonder!'
>
> And I, when he stretched out his arm to me,
> fixed my eyes on his baked aspect, so that the
> scorching of his visage hindered not
>
> my mind from knowing him; and bending my
> face to his, I answered: 'Are you here, Ser
> Brunetto?'[5]

No verse form in English literature is more closely associated with its originator than *terza rima* with Dante. It is difficult to imagine a mature poet using that form without the 'feeling of profound kinship' that Eliot describes and, in *Little Gidding*, proudly proclaims. The ghost he meets in his modern Inferno is compounded of Yeats and others. Eliot was at pains to stress the *others* since, as he told John Hayward: 'I do not wish to take the responsibility of putting Yeats or anybody else into Hell and I do not want to impute to him the particular vice [sodomy] which took Brunetto there.' Eliot had reviewed Yeats's *Last Poems* in 1940 and, only a year later, writing *Little Gidding*, presumably remembered the poem 'Cuchulain Comforted', in which Yeats on his death-bed used *terza rima* – for the first and last time – to articulate a Dantesque dream of death. Its setting is a wood, and *Little Gidding* suggests another memory of Dante's 'dark wood', but it is a memory of a memory. Eliot's 'dead leaves' blown by the 'dawn wind' are the 'leaves dead . . . driven, like ghosts from an enchanter fleeing,' by the West Wind of Shelley's Ode. Those leaves have blown a long way: from The Book of Isaiah (34:4) by way of the *Iliad* (VI, 146–8), the *Aeneid* (VI, 309–10), the *Divine Comedy* (*Inferno*, III, 112–15), and *Paradise Lost* (I, 301–4). Eliot's leaves and Shelley's blow from the same tree and provide a further illustration of the relationship I proposed between poems by Herbert, Keats, and Byron: the form, the cadence, carrying the theme.

The 'Ode to the West Wind' also offers another illustration of that 'feeling of profound kinship, or rather of a peculiar personal intimacy, with another, probably a dead author' of which Eliot speaks. Shelley's Ode is in *terza rima* and, in case his reader should overlook that signal, he added a note that begins: 'This poem was conceived and chiefly written in a wood that skirts the Arno, near Florence.' In a wood outside Dante's city, Shelley asks the wind that Dante breathed to inspire him. Far from exhibiting the anxiety of influence, the Ode is a prayer – to the wind, to Dante – *for* influence. The ghost of *Little Gidding* says

> our concern was speech, and speech impelled us
> To purify the dialect of the tribe . . . .

The ghost of Yeats's 'Cuchulain Comforted' is told 'Now must we sing and sing the best we can', and poem after poem in Dante's *terza rima* follows him in its concern with language, 'the dialect of the tribe', the *'vulgare illustre'*, the noble vernacular.

Let me now turn to a poem which no one, so far as I am aware, has ever suggested has anything to do with Dante, Philip Larkin's 'Talking in Bed':

> Talking in bed ought to be easiest,
> Lying together there goes back so far,
> An emblem of two people being honest.
>
> Yet more and more time passes silently.
> Outside, the wind's incomplete unrest
> Builds and disperses clouds about the sky,
>
> And dark towns heap up on the horizon.
> None of this cares for us. Nothing shows why
> At this unique distance from isolation
>
> It becomes still more difficult to find
> Words at once true and kind,
> Or not untrue and not unkind.

This, too, is concerned with language, words true and untrue, but what else might connect it with Dante? Our first impression that it is written in *terza rima* proves to be wrong. We expect the 4th and 6th lines to rhyme with the 2nd, but they do not: instead, the 5th line rhymes with the 1st and 3rd, and so on. We might call this *terza rima* upside down. Why should it be so? Let me leave that question hanging for the moment and return to the poem. It opens in a bedroom: 'Lying together there goes back so far'. As far as the Garden of Eden, that Dante found on the summit of the mountain of purgatory. In Larkin's post-lapsarian world, 'more and more time passes silently'; the lovers telling fewer lies to each other, or lying without speaking, and time itself passing inaudibly. Outside the bedroom, a wind blows clouds, I think from Shelley's Ode, and dark towns heap up like leaves.

> None of this cares for us. Nothing shows why
> At this unique distance from isolation
>
> It becomes still more difficult to find
> Words at once true and kind,
> Or not untrue and not unkind.

Words for what? For the unspoken subject of the poem, the proclaimed subject of Dante's poem: Love. The *Divine Comedy* celebrates cosmic order, unity, union, where Larkin can only celebrate love cooling on a cooling star under the shadow of isolation and the void. Dante's universe has been turned upside down, so his *terza rima* must follow suit.

In his book *The Pastoral Art of Robert Frost* (1960), John F. Lynen says: 'Frost's sentences are always clear, his verse forms traditional, his language close to everyday speech – no obscurity here, no oblique glances at Dante.' The American poet may have traditional luggage, but it contains nothing smuggled from Europe. Reading 'Stopping by Woods on a Snowy Evening', I wonder:

> Whose woods these are I think I know.
> His house is in the village, though;
> He will not see me stopping here
> To watch his woods fill up with snow.
>
> My little horse must think it queer
> To stop without a farmhouse near
> Between the woods and frozen lake
> The darkest evening of the year.
>
> He gives his harness bells a shake
> To ask if there is some mistake.
> The only other sound's the sweep
> Of easy wind and downy flake.
>
> The woods are lovely, dark, and deep,
> But I have promises to keep,
> And miles to go before I sleep,
> And miles to go before I sleep.

No *terza rima* here; tetrameters rather than pentameters; but that interlaced rhyme-scheme has a familiar air, and what is the poem about? Someone who, in the middle of a journey, comes to woods that are 'lovely, dark, and deep'. 'Whose woods these are I think I know.' Let me remind you how the *Divine Comedy* opens (in the English translation that I believe Frost had read):

> In the middle of the journey of our life I came
>   to myself in a dark wood where the straight
>   way was lost.

Ah! how hard a thing it is to tell what a wild,
   and rough, and stubborn wood this was, which
   in my thought renews the fear!
So bitter is it, that scarcely more is death: but
   to treat of the good that I there found, I will
   relate the other things that I discerned.
I cannot rightly tell how I entered it, so full of
   sleep was I about the moment that I left the
   true way.
But after I had reached the foot of a Hill there,
   where that valley ended, which had pierced
   my heart with fear,
I looked up and saw its shoulders already clothed
   with the rays of the Planet that leads men
   straight on every road.
Then the fear was somewhat calmed, which had
   continued in the lake of my heart the night
   that I passed so piteously.[6]

Is Frost's poem not another dream-transformation? Again, I suspect a subliminal memory mistaken for annunciation; a memory of interlaced stanzas bringing into a new configuration Dante's dark wood and lake, Shelley's 'wind and downy flake' (leaf metamorphosed into snowflake). At the centre of Frost's poem – as of Keats's ballad 'La Belle Dame' – is an unvoiced perception of the death named in the earlier texts of Dante and Herbert. And true to the tradition of *terza rima*, language is ranged against death: 'I have *promises* to keep' – promises to himself, to poetry, to those that read poetry. 'Stopping by Woods' is the fulfilment of such a promise.

Let me turn now from the poet's experience of creating a poem to the reader's experience of *re*-creating it. It is generally agreed that the pleasure and profit to be had from poetry is not so much in reading it as in *re*-reading it; just as the pleasure to be had from music is in hearing a piece that we like again and again. Music and poetry have much in common. The more we hear them, the more we enjoy them and the more we remember them. Remembering them, we can enjoy them without a book, without a tape. But how many poems can we enjoy – can our children enjoy – without a book? Our children probably have by heart the words of more songs than we do, but fewer poems. I have a theory regarding the role of poetry in society that I am tempted to call Stallworthy's Law. We know that in most primitive societies poetry plays a crucial role in its association with religion, ritual, magic. The poet as shaman makes way for the poet as historian, the poet as entertainer. Then comes the book, the radio, the television, the video. It is argued that, with quick access to libraries and tapes, no one needs to *learn* poems any more, with the result that when they are read, they are mostly read – like everything else – with the eye alone; seldom with the ear. Stallworthy's Law maintains that, the more technologically developed a society, the more marginal will be the place of poetry. Certainly, if you look at the United States, the United Kingdom, Ireland, the Soviet Union – or, at any rate, as *I* look at them – this seems to be the case. Seamus Heaney will be known, and his poems will be known, *less* widely in Ireland than Yevtushenko and his poems are known in Russia; but *more* widely than the Poet Laureate and his poems are known in England. And when you cross the Atlantic you see – or when *I* cross the Atlantic, I think *I* see – poetry almost everywhere driven off the streets and living comfortably, perhaps too comfortably, in colleges and universities.

Is this unfair? Perhaps a little, but no one could say that the English-speaking peoples – inheritors of a language with the richest poetic literature the world has ever known – are getting the full benefit of their inheritance. And if one is disturbed by the prospect of that literature playing an ever more marginal role in the lives of one's children and grandchildren, one must ask oneself whether the trend is irreversible. The answer is surely no, and the next question is the Russian one: *What is to be Done*? The 1987 Nobel prizewinner for Literature offers a Russian answer. Joseph Brodsky writes in his essay 'A Guide to a Renamed City':

> there is the second Petersburg, the one made of verses and of Russian prose. That prose is read and re-read and the verses are learned by heart, if only because in Soviet schools children are

made to memorize them if they want to graduate. And it's this memorization which secures the city's status and place in the future – as long as this language exists – and transforms the Soviet school-children into the Russian people.

That question and that answer seem worth discussing at a time when our educational priorities and curricula are under review. I can already hear the voices objecting to forced feeding, but does feeding have to be forced? Most children in this country are introduced to poetry – in the form of nursery rhymes – as they are beginning to talk. They enjoy them and learn them effortlessly. Then they go to pre-school play groups, and from there to school and, in many cases, little more is heard of poetry until it is introduced as a rather remote and difficult topic several years later. If, however, there were to be no interruption, and children progressed from nursery rhymes at home to nonsense verse, light verse, and some more serious at primary school; if they were taught to read poems simultaneously with the eye and the ear, and if they were taught to memorize poems, I believe that many more English-speaking children would come into their poetic inheritance than do now. What effect would this have on their lives? Let me turn again to the Russian experience. In Heinrich Böll's Preface to Eugenia Ginzburg's book *Within the Whirlwind* (1981), an account of her years as a prisoner in Siberian labour camps, he writes:

Although I have some knowledge of the Gulag Archipelago, my interest as I read this book never for an instant wavered, and this may be partly because this astonishing woman has never lost her sense of humor, never mislaid it during her enforced wanderings when she was shunted about between a number of hells and a few dots of 'heaven'. That in itself would be a miracle. And a further miracle is – here one can only stand in awe – that she has poetry to thank for her strength and endurance, her will to survive in even the most hopeless situations. As soon as she has but a few minutes' peace and quiet, is able to breathe, to sit, lie, take a deep breath, lines of poetry come into her mind and across her lips: Akhmatova, Pasternak, Mandelstam, as well as novels, stories, literature – in other words, everything a Russian woman of her time simply carries *with her*; a possession that cannot be confiscated, that survives all the searches . . . .

When Eugenia Ginzburg meets her son Vasya again after twelve years [a son last seen when he was four], she recites poems to him during the night; he carries on where she leaves off, and that is how she 'recognizes' him.

We should never underestimate the power of Mnemosyne, mother of the Muses, and the power of her daughter, Poetry.

Notes

1 As related in Cicero, *De Oratore*, II, lxxxvi, 351–4.
2 H. Bloom, *The Anxiety of Influence: A Theory of Poetry*, New York: Oxford University Press, 1973; *A Map of Misreading*, New York: Oxford University Press, 1975; *Kabbalah and Criticism*, New York: The Seabury Press, 1975; and *Poetry and Repression: Revisionism from Blake to Stevens*, New Haven, Conn.: Yale University Press, 1976.
3 *The Anxiety of Influence*, p. 30.
4 C. Ricks, Review of Helen Gardner: *The Composition of Four Quartets*, London: Faber & Faber, 1978, in the *Times Literary Supplement*, 15 Sept. 1978, p. 1008.
5 *The Inferno of Dante Aligheri*, tr. J. A. Carlyle, 2nd edn 1867, revised H. Oelsner, London: J. M. Dent, 1900, reset 1932, pp. 159–61.
6 Ibid., p. 3.

8

Heritage and Danger: The English Past in the Era of the Welfare State

Patrick Wright

In the summer of 1987 the design company Pentagram mounted an exhibition at the Royal Academy. The moving spirit was Theo Crosby, a South African-born architect who is interiors director with Pentagram, and his model showed a monument to the Battle of Britain that he would like to see built in the Docklands area of London. Pentagram issued two suitably stylish black booklets in which Crosby argued his case and outlined a broader vision of the 'new Jerusalem' that London might at last become.[1]

The first strand in Crosby's argument was cultural. There had, as he suggested, been disastrous problems with the peace that broke out after the Second World War. Modernist thinking took over and ' "useful" short term strategies' like schools and hospitals were given priority over 'long term monuments and civic ornaments'. This ' "liberal" decision' played into the hands of experts who were pleased to close ranks behind an 'ideology that gave them scope to experiment and a blissful freedom from personal responsibility'. It also 'broke a thread leading back three thousand years'. Only now, after the humiliation of the reforming state which did such damage to our cities and national character, is 'the necessity of monuments' coming to be appreciated once again: the monument as a marker and 'urban instrument'. The 1980s are a 'miraculous' time: a time of 'Beginnings' in which the 'ideal city' can be rediscovered amidst all the mediocre confusion of post-war London. Art and skill can be built back into the fabric of the city. The rule of Style can be reasserted over a building technology which has been allowed to run rampant. Crosby's monument is a memorial, but it is also proposed as the spiritual lever with which we can prevent ourselves from sinking any further into the post-war swamp.

If this was the cultural justification for Crosby's monument, it was accompanied by a commercial one. The failure of vision which lasted throughout the post-war period of massive urban expansion has left us with no monuments except those that already existed in the old and historic urban centres. Meanwhile, tourism is booming and the British are squaring up their new destiny as 'a nation of shopkeepers become hoteliers'. Fifteen million people visit London every year, and this figure – as Crosby projects – could well have doubled by the year 2000. Old attractions like the Tower of London and Westminster Abbey are stretched to capacity and there is a growing problem of 'through-put'. Along with new monuments, there should be public education programmes designed to build people's architectural awareness. Unemployment 'will inevitably increase', after all, and it will not just be visiting tourists who have time to practise their interpretative skills as they wander the themed-up streets of the re-idealized city.

Crosby's Battle of Britain monument claims its place in a city which must be redeveloped if it is to thrive in a post-industrial, 'leisure'-orientated future. The Thames is deindustrializing fast – a greening of the river which is not quite of the sort imagined by William Morris in *News From Nowhere* – and if Crosby has his way it will soon be restored to its proper pride of place as the capital's most significant thoroughfare. Busy with upgraded tourist amenities, the river will become the source of meaning, and the ideal city which flows from it will extend along two 'axes' which Crosby has worked up out of existing heritage imagery. Running across a loop of the river from Westminster Abbey to St. Paul's, the 'Canaletto Axis' derives from that famous view, painted from the Terrace of Somerset House, of the City of London huddling under Wren's dome while a hundred more modest spires indicate further transcendence to the east. The 'Turner axis', which also has a canvas origin, comes down from Greenwich, crossing the river twice and touching the Tower before it too culminates at St. Paul's.

There is presently, so Crosby says, a dearth of monuments along these axes; and there must be more if the city is to be grand once again. Some are already under construction – the Globe Shakespeare Centre, the Design Museum, the recycled Battersea Power Station – but Docklands remains a desert: a 'vast space, destroyed more by peace and changing technology than war'. Of course, development is underway but 'the general effect is restless, temporary, small-scale . . . nothing with aspirations beyond private comfort and corporate greed'. So it is here – in this tormented place which cries out for 'an antidote, a great marker, a communal beacon; a civic gesture' – that the Battle of Britain monument should stand. Once again, as Crosby promises (with a sub-Heideggerean utterance which he attributes mistakenly to Gertrude Stein), 'there will be a there there'.

What of the monument itself? Crosby insists that it will be touched with 'aboriginal innocence' of the sort that has previously drawn tourists to more primitive places. He also promises, somewhat more predictably, that it will give visitors 'a dose of the right stuff'. The base takes the form of the 'original tomb': a pyramid with an arched entrance, a 'cave' which is entered between Doric Columns. The hollow interior is haunted by holograms and moving images – ghosts which 'come whisperingly to life on arrival and die away as the visitor leaves'. A vertical ghost train carries the visitor up through the strata of London's war. Subterranean images of shelters, tubes, control rooms and bunkers give way to a ground-level display of collapsing houses, fire wardens and anti-aircraft guns. At the top are the fighters, bombers and barrage balloons of the airborne drama.

Externally, the pyramid is 'rusticated, clad in granite'. A twenty-foot-high frieze tells the story of the war, from Dunkirk to the surrender on Luneberg Heath. Cut in stone above this are words from Winston Churchill's most celebrated wartime speech ('We shall fight them on the beaches . . .').[2] The tower soars up from the pyramid and is covered with 'symbols of regeneration and memory'. Six-metre-high sculptures of the Aviators are placed at the corners of the upper stage, and the figures of 'women, helpers and mourners' stand between them. At this point, the tower twists to create 'diagonal lattices which light the figures and the pyramid roof'. Visitors step out of glass lifts which have brought them up the outside of the tower at vertiginous speed, and steady themselves on an upper platform some 500 feet above ground. They look over East London: 'a battlefield of the war and a casualty of the peace'. Tombs and sepulchres offer shelter from the weather, while the glass walls are engraved with stories of the Blitz and descriptions of visible landmarks. Searchlights placed in the tombs illuminate the upper levels and 'orchestrate a dance, a cathedral of light in the sky'. After witnessing this bizarre tribute to both London Blitz and Nuremberg Rally, visitors will reach the 'final experience, the sacred place high in the vast sky'. A sculpture by Michael Sandle will show 'a circular pit with chairs and a table set with a simple meal, a corpse laid out'. Above this 'sombre scene', a Heinkel bomber crashes down through a disintegrating cathedral, while a 'tiny Spitfire fighter hurtles through beside it'. The visitor to this 'place of national pilgrimage' is expected to suffer vertigo and visual surprise, the rapid ascent in those externally placed glass lifts forming 'a major element in the experience of visiting'.

Crosby costs his monument at £30 million – about the same, he notes, as a single Harrier or Tornado jet – and he is certainly not looking for a government subsidy. Visitors pay at the door, and the monument would be 'a perfectly viable commercial investment'. In conversation with journalists he has also animated the project in autobiographical terms and answered some of his critics. As he told Martin Pawley, 'I was in the war, I had a great time.' The design is indeed influenced by Albert Speer and Wilhelm Krier, but the classical style is now emerging from its totalitarian deformation: 'I should have thought that everybody now accepts that in the war the Germans were good chaps just like us who fought like tigers. Anyway I think it's time we got back some of the inheritance we lost just because Hitler happened to like Classical architecture.' As for Docklands, this 'used to be a wonderful place, but it has no spiritual content. That's why we put the monument there . . . it's amazing how empty most people's lives are, they really have nothing but TV and video. What we need for our own safety as much as anything else is real cultural monuments so there is a public presence in the streets.[3]

Theo Crosby's monument combines 'B'-movie methods of memorialization with the money-making exhilaration of the big dipper and the stern social purpose of an exercise in community policing. At present there are no plans to build it, and Crosby himself is apparently not seeking to raise the funds. But even if the story ends with Pentagram's model, Crosby's monument has already made a number of significant points. To start with, it has asserted very clearly that the idea of 'heritage' need not always stand in opposition to development. It has been the practice since Victorian times to defend what is understood as 'heritage' against the ravages of modernization, but in recent years the idea has been turning up in the vanguard of one urban development scheme after the next.[4] Here, then, from a company that is in the forefront of the much-vaunted 'design revolution', is another version of the 'post-modern' offer. Where previously there was only conflict and antagonism, a new synthesis is now proposed: we really can have both tradition *and* modernization, memory *and* the new Beginning, heritage *and* the most extensive redevelopment imaginable. Crosby's monument appeared to corroborate the theorists of 'hyper-reality' who have argued that in a world governed by 'simulation', history finally disappears into its own televisual image and the real thing can no longer be distinguished from the 'absolute fake'.[5] But, as it turned out, there were some partisans of old-fashioned memory who wanted nothing to do with this kind of memorialization. The Association of Battle of Britain Pilots took one look at Pentagram's model and, after denouncing it as 'unsuitable' and 'an insult to those who died', insisted that a proper statue of Air Chief Marshal Lord Dowding, Commander-in-Chief of Fighter Command in 1940, would be altogether more appropriate. Dowding himself had apparently eyed an empty plinth in Trafalgar Square – joking that it was 'reserved for me, but much later!' – and in April 1988 the *Sunday Telegraph* surveyed its readers and declared Lord Dowding the favourite contender for this still-vacant position of national honour. By this time, however, the long-overdue statue for which the memory of Lord Dowding had been obliged to

wait nearly fifty years was announced for a different site: the
Queen Mother would be unveiling it the following October at
the RAF church of St. Clement Danes.[6]

The rise of a modern past

Theo Crosby is not merely eccentric in his vision of London. A
comparable return to the ideal city was advocated by Prince
Charles in his celebrated Mansion House speech on the subject of
Paternoster Square. The Prince never claimed that the Germans
fought like tigers, but he did prefer the Luftwaffe's rubble to the
dismal buildings which were thrown up around St. Paul's in the
years of post-war reconstruction. Condemning the 'deep aesthetic
idleness which has afflicted the post-war world' and placing the
blame firmly on Attlee's 1947 Town and Country Planning Act,
he too cited Canaletto's London skyline as the vision to which
the City should return.[7] Like Crosby's monument, the Prince's
speech rehearsed a characteristically schematic interpretation of
British history since 1940. The post-war years are taken as a
single span or period of memory, and then arranged according to
a narrative structure which has all the simplicity of a fable. First
there was the war – that moment of unity and sacrifice in which
'we' proved and defended our true national identity against
enormous odds. Then there was the peace which 'broke out', in a
phrase of Angela Thirkell's, and became far more destructive
than the war itself.[8] Now in the 1980s, and after a decade in
which hope seemed finally to die, comes the miraculous moment
of revival when the war is recovered and redeclared, a superior
memory, against the pernicious peace that followed it.

Versions of this revivalist fable seem currently to be playing in
every sphere of the national culture. The arts are going the way
of ale and becoming 'real' again.[9] Proper figures are rushing back
into our sadly abstracted painting, architects are remembering
how to build proper homes and poetry has started to make sense,
even to rhyme again. Often presented as if it were another Battle
of Britain fought against overwhelming odds, this return to 'real'
culture is actually very much in the grain of the times. While
formerly pampered modernists everywhere shuffle off into the

wings, a whole company of long-neglected heroes are brought forward, often posthumously, and congratulated for their stand. Here, once again, are 'the few' who put up with neglect and derision in the dark age of modernization and social reform: figures like Lutyens and Erith in architecture, Betjeman and Larkin in poetry, John Piper and other members of the retrospectively assembled 'neo-romantic' school in painting. Here also is the post-war metaphor of treason and the betrayed world of John Le Carré's Circus, peopled as it is by superior characters who have been overtaken by the lesser systems-men of the modern state. Cuckolded, on the bottle in North Oxford, or skulking in some makeshift teaching position at a preparatory school, the old guard may have gone to seed, but they are still capable of tracking down a truth that would otherwise be lost to the world. The variations on this theme are many, but all of them elaborate a polarized opposition between modernity and the old ways of the nation: an opposition which itself stands among the most significant features of post-war British culture.

The British past – efflorescent as it now is – has risen in response to the problems and anxieties of the post-war era, and its development can be traced from 1945. Theo Crosby may regret that no one built a monument to mark the Battle of Britain, but at the time 1945 seemed to be its own miraculous year. Formed after the election victory of 26 July, the Attlee government promised a new idea of the nation, confident that enlightened social reform could be achieved through the state. Tradition was a hindrance that could be overcome, and history was a matter of progress, of looking forward rather than back. Intractable social problems would be tackled by the new institutions of the welfare state. The economy would not just be mixed; it would be pushed, prodded and squeezed until it delivered prosperity. The very soil of the nation would be revitalized as public policy reformed the wasteful traditions of the private farm.

For the brief moment that it lasted, this vision of a renewed and transformed nation offered a far greater tribute to the war effort than any more conventional memorial might have done. But Attlee's was not the only utopia on offer in 1945. Evelyn

Waugh's *Brideshead Revisited* was also published in 1945. While
Attlee's vision was full of future promise, Waugh's faced the
other way and paid its tribute to a superior and traditional
England, idealized and saluted 'at the moment of extinction'.[10]
Brideshead was already only a memory – a place of classical
fountains and white raspberries, of mahogany-framed bathtubs
and rounds of halma played with Nanny Hawkins – which has
slipped sadly out of kilter with the present order of things. The
family had disintegrated and the ancestral house was suffering
rough treatment at the hands of an occupying army which
claimed, absurdly enough, to be on the same side. Its picturesque
wooded valley – planned and planted in the eighteenth century
'so that, at about this date, it might be seen in its maturity' – was
just entering service as an assault course and mortar range, and
the prospect was dismal. Others beside Waugh were similarly
concerned. Introducing a book on *The English Country House* in
1935, the mine-owning Osbert Sitwell sounded a gloomy note
from Renishaw Hall near Sheffield:[11]

> Alas! How curious it is that these works of art only begin to
> obtain a wide appreciation when they are on the verge of being
> destroyed. . . . What country houses of any size, one wonders,
> can hope to survive the next fifty years? . . . And, indeed, as I sit
> writing these lines in an old house, I recall that two great houses
> in the neighbourhood have been dismantled and gutted within the
> last few years.

Dornford Yates also wrote a novel on this theme. *The House
that Berry Built* was published in January 1945 and it told of
White Ladies, a country house in Hampshire which, for
predictable reasons, had been signed over to the nation in 1937.[12]
With their ancestral home now in use as 'an official retreat for the
Secretary of State for Foreign Affairs', the Pleydell family move
to the Pyrenees where they discover a 'little, English meadow,
locked in the arms of France' and, using their own cultural
instinct rather than the superficial expertise of professional
architects, set about rebuilding the house which could no longer
be sustained in the deteriorated nation which had once been

home.[13] The war was one problem, but even before this a
General Election – described as 'probably the finest argument for
dictatorship the world had ever seen' – had brought people into
the cabinet who 'would not have qualified for the reference
traditionally accorded to the incompetent charwoman'. For
Dornford Yates, who was rarely short of an explanation where a
convenient Jew or Communist could be found, the truth had
been 'swamped' and the country rendered uninhabitable by political manipulation, betrayal and the rise of Parliamentary socialism.

But despite these dire warnings, the total levelling of the old
ancestral nation never quite took place. There were many sad
losses, but the securing of the country house against the taxing
drift of post-war times stands, without doubt, as a major cultural
achievement of the last fifty years. In the pre-war world of
Brideshead Revisited, the 'Georgian Society' can only protest
hopelessly as fine old houses all round the country are razed to
make way for new 'blocks of flats'. But by the late 1940s a
considerably more effective lobby was stating its case against a
reforming government which had already started to stumble. As
preservationist bodies worked to save the country house, they
also assisted in its rebirth as a powerful cultural symbol.
Cultivated as a quotation from a supposedly grander age, the
country house sparkled with new and distinctly contemporary
significance as it was played off against the grey prose of the
post-war settlement surrounding it. Just as the medieval heaven
needed the horrors of hell to keep its contrastingly celestial
features clear, the preserved country house has come to depend
on a sense of all-encompassing threat for its own clarity of
definition. We will not understand its contemporary meaning
unless we look beyond the noble edifice which has absorbed so
much celebratory attention over the last four decades, and
consider the dark portrayals of danger massed in its shadows.

By 1948 *Country Life* was describing its own project on the
back of the guidebooks which it published for the National
Trust:[14]

In a famous phrase Canning spoke of 'recalling the New World
. . . to redress the balance of the old.' It is not a mere play on

words to claim that one of the constant endeavours of *Country Life*, in these restless and changeable times, is to recall the Old World to redress the balance of the New . . . *Country Life* believes that the present cannot dispense with the cumulative wisdom of the past; that unless progress and tradition go hand in hand, and good taste is preserved, there is a grave danger of destroying the good with the bad in our efforts to rebuild Britain.

Founded in the 1890s, The National Trust has a long familiarity with the polar opposition between 'heritage' and 'danger'. But while 'heritage' has been among its keywords since the early days (Hardwicke Rawnsley, a founder of the Trust, published a book called *A Nation's Heritage* in 1920), the definition has undergone considerable change. The Trust spent its early decades securing a public and national interest in land and small buildings threatened by destructive private ownership. Public access was a central issue, taken over to a considerable extent from the Commons Preservation Society, and for Rawnsley at least the founding vision was of a body that would hold culturally significant landscapes in the public interest: 'a great National Gallery of natural pictures', as he put it at an early meeting.[15] The large country house didn't become an issue for the National Trust until 1934, when Lord Lothian addressed the Annual General Meeting on this emerging theme. At this time, according to a book published to celebrate the Trust's fiftieth anniversary in 1945, the Trust only owned two such buildings – Montacute and Barrington Court. By 1945 the number had risen to 17.[16] At the time of writing the figure stands at 87. In 1942 the Trust's membership stood at 6000 and its paid staff at six people. By now its membership is over one and a half million and the staff – excluding volunteers and people working on government funded job-creation schemes run by the Trust – stands at about 2000. The growth and re-orientation of the National Trust as it rose to the new challenge of the country house stands among the most characteristic developments of the welfare state era.

In 1936, and at the suggestion of Vita Sackville-West, James Lees-Milne was employed by the National Trust as historic buildings secretary. He was responsible for developing the new

Country Houses Scheme, and his published diaries, together with his autobiographical writings, offer a quite remarkable picture of the country house in the early years of its re-establishment as a preserved object.

Lees-Milne experienced the polarity between heritage and danger in deeply autobiographical terms. He had grown up in the timeless tranquillity of Whickhamford Manor near Evesham, and was raised – if this is the appropriate word to use of a person who seems rather to have wandered up like a rambling Victorian rose – by parents of a sporting and philistine kind. In *Another Self*, an autobiography published in 1970, Lees-Milne recalls the manor as a sacred place of childhood: 'Like all children,' he writes, 'I knew intimately every corner, the squeak of every board, the latch of every cupboard of my home. Each room had its peculiar smell, its own light or dark personality, its own strong ethos.'[17] This fondly remembered home offers itself as a model of the national heritage which would need preserving in subsequent years, and the sense of threat was also there in the financial insecurity of the Lees-Milne family. James Lees-Milne would inherit the right kinds of memory, but like the Pleydell family in Dornford Yates's novel, he wouldn't get the means to keep the story going. From the beginning, everything that mattered – history, nation and culture – were cherished in direct relation to a vividly imagined threat of dispossession.

A primary theme in Lees-Milne's autobiography, this threat of dispossession takes on wider dimensions as the story is developed. James's father couldn't send his son to Cambridge, apparently because he himself still owed money from his own time there. And Oxford had been ruled out ever since his father had heard that there were 'three niggers at Balliol'. Earlier proof that the world was falling out of joint had been provided by the General Strike of 1926. Lees-Milne senior studied the signs of the times and decided that the game was up: 'We must all learn to stand on our own feet now.' Since the approaching Revolution would be 'Bolshevik and bloody', he bought in a huge supply of ammunition, took to polishing up his shot-guns and stalking rifles, and – with the help of a pitchfork and a stuffed sack hung up specially for the purpose in a mulberry tree – introduced young James to the mysteries of the bayonet.

After a bizarre detour through a secretarial college for young ladies, James Lees-Milne finally arrived at Oxford, and it was here that the polarity between heritage and danger would be appropriately confirmed. One summer evening Lees-Milne was taken to Rousham, a Jacobean house on the river Cherwell which, at the time, was leased to a 'capricious alcoholic' who liked to entertain undergraduates. As he got into his stride this fellow started whipping the family portraits (Knellers and Reynoldses) with a riding crop so that the paint flaked off. He then went out onto the terrace with a gun and started blasting away at the private parts of the statues which had been set in the garden in the 1740s by William Kent. James Lees-Milne recalls this evening as 'a turning point' in his life:

> It brought home to me how passionately I cared for architecture and the continuity of history, of which it was the mouthpiece. I felt sick as many people would feel sick if they watched from a train window an adult torturing a child, while they were powerless to intervene. Those Rococo rooms at Rousham, with their delicate furniture, and portraits of bewigged, beribboned ancestors, were living, palpable children to me. They and the man-fashioned landscape outside were the England that mattered. I suddenly saw them as infinitely fragile and precious. They meant to me then, and have meant ever since, far more than human lives. They represent the things of the spirit. And the ghastly truth is that like humans, they are not perdurable.

Lees-Milne recalls making a secret resolution after that evening: 'I vowed that I would devote my energies and abilities, such as they were, to preserving the country houses of England.'[18]

If there is love in one paragraph there must – according to the romantic structure of feeling governing this autobiography – be hatred in the next. As Lees-Milne comments, 'Hatred is deemed to be a great sin; but it can be a salutary emotion, a cleanser of the spirit.' And since 'one cannot love without hating', the second thing that Oxford did for Lees-Milne ('and beyond the two I can think of no others') was to provide him with a proper object for his hatred: not wealthy vandals like the man at Rousham who wreck works of art, but Communism which does the same for the entire human spirit.

This is what happened to the country house and the ways of life associated with it in the post-war period. In the eye of the preservationist, as well as the novelist and neo-romantic painter, it came to be loved and cherished in the same measure that other vividly imagined tendencies in the world were loathed and hated. In the 1930s Lees-Milne was a Franco-supporting romantic of decidedly reactionary opinion. A maverick who calls himself far more right-wing than Tory, he condemned Churchill for falling in love with war and allowing a war of principle to degenerate into a war between nations. The destruction of Germany, with its historic seats of learning, should never have taken place, and the Soviet occupation of Eastern Europe was its direct consequence. As the war comes to an end, James Lees-Milne hopes the peace will only be a short respite before hostilities are renewed against the real enemy in the Soviet Union. A conveniently all-purpose demon at the best of times, the spectre of Communism would offer an obliging gloss for post-war social democracy after Peace broke out in 1945.

As historic buildings secretary Lees-Milne cycled or drove around the country in the National Trust's faltering Austin, visiting house after house and bizarre owner after bizarre owner, returning to London to lunch at Brooks or the White Tower and then going home – perhaps via the Courtauld Institute where Kenneth Clark was delivering a lecture – to Cheyne Walk to pen an article for *Country Life*. Meanwhile the polarity between heritage and danger was proliferating luxuriously in his diary. Initially content to value the survival of buildings over that of people, it went on to establish a more inclusive opposition between the traditional *nation* and the degenerate modern *society* which, after the war, was threatening to replace it. The Communist menace was certainly still abroad, but its domestic equivalent emerged shortly after Churchill gave way to Attlee in 1945.

The instinctive aristocratic culture and naturalized social hierarchy embodied by the country house were quickly lined up against the false enlightenment of 1945. Lees-Milne viewed the democracy of the 'little people' with scarcely disguised contempt, and he scorned attempts to harness the country house to the cause of social democratic reform. In March 1948, for example, Lees-Milne visited Attingham Park in Shropshire, where George Trevelyan was setting up an adult education college, and his comments are typical: 'A little folk-dancing, some social economy and Fabianism for the miners and their wives. We felt quite sick from the nonsense of it all. At a time when this country is supposed to be bankrupt they spend [our] money on semi-education of the lower classes who will merely learn from it to be dissatisfied. The house looked very forlorn and down at heel which worried me a good deal.'[19]

This polarity between traditional nation and modern society set the private values of the aristocratic house off against the public egalitarian tendencies of the reforming present. It set the ancestral continuities of the aristocratic family off against social democratic ideas of citizenship. It set high national culture off against the procedural and bureaucratic realities of the modern state. Quickly enough, it also developed a territorial dimension. Some areas had been lost forever and in these no one should expect to find the traditional nation at all. The East End of London was clearly one such place. In April 1946, ten years after he was first employed as historic buildings secretary, Lees-Milne made his first visit to what has remained the Trust's only property in the East End of London. Sutton House had been restored in 1936 after George Lansbury – Poplar councillor, Labour MP for Bow and Bromley, erstwhile leader of the Labour Party and at the time also a Vice-President of the National Trust – had launched a public appeal in *The Times*.[20] The appeal declared Sutton House to be among the 'finest secular buildings in the East End of London' and insisted that it should somehow be preserved for 'public and social services' in the district. Given the new priorities of the Country Houses Scheme, Lees-Milne saw nothing of interest here. In his view, this building, which John Summerson had identified as a 'composition of fragmentary beauties welded together in the course of time', was 'wretched' and 'no more important than hundreds of other

Georgian houses still left in slum areas. Very derelict after the bombing all around it. . . . It does have one downstairs room of linenfold panelling. I found it terribly depressing and longed to hurry away.'[21] Bombs may not have been so absolutely good for these slums as they were for Betjeman's unrelievedly modern Slough, but with the true nation beleaguered and needing assistance in the Shires, Sutton House could be abandoned to the municipal oblivion that was already engulfing it. When Lees-Milne prepared the National Trust guide to its buildings in 1948, Sutton House was not among the properties he chose to mention.[22]

From the beginning, then, the National Trust's entirely proper concern that grand historic buildings and their collections should be preserved in the public interest was accompanied by a frankly reactionary assessment of post-war social and political developments. Since then the Trust has emerged from the margins of public life and become a major force in the national culture. Resymbolized, the country house has become more secure than could ever have been imagined in the dark days of the 1930s and 1940s. Disaster may certainly still loom for individual buildings, but the overall picture has improved beyond measure. By 1959, as Marcus Binney and Gervase Jackson-Stops have pointed out, Evelyn Waugh expressed happy surprise at the survival of these apparently doomed buildings, admitting in a new Preface that he had 'piled it on rather' when writing *Brideshead Revisited*. Ralph Dutton's book on *The English Country House* was reprinted in 1962, and a similar although unacknowledged adjustment ensured that Osbert Sitwell's 1935 Foreword had quietly lost the gloomy concluding paragraph quoted earlier.

Of course there has been movement in the National Trust and it would be wrong to identify the policy of the organization which the Trust has become with the attitudes of the young Lees-Milne. Recognizing how deeply it has been influenced by the crisis and subsequent cult of the country house, the Trust has gone out to recover and reassert some of its pre-war priorities. Thus, for example, the coastline project Enterprise Neptune was launched in 1963 and relaunched in 1985 as part of a deliberate attempt to widen the Trust's image from its identification with the country house. But continuities have also developed as some of the reflexes of the early Country Houses Scheme have gone on to find a broader social resonance in the 1970s and 1980s. Thus, for example, while the sense of emergency which characterized the Trust's early rescue endeavours has become the conventional rhetoric of a well-tried and effective system of acquisition – alarmed letters in *The Times*, vigorous Parliamentary lobbying, the appalled invocation of 'our endangered heritage' etc. – it has also started to function as a wider metaphor of social decline. The stately homes line up, one after the next, on the brink of the abyss, and each time the country knows that it is going to the dogs. In this way the Mentmore fiasco became emblematic of a Labour government's general incompetence in 1977. But the polarity between 'heritage' and 'danger' had become frankly political by 1974 when Roy Strong and Marcus Binney mounted their exhibition on 'The Destruction of the Country House' at the Victoria and Albert Museum. Here, as Robert Hewison has recently pointed out, was a direct response to a Labour government contemplating the introduction of a wealth tax.[23]

The preserved country house also supports a new kind of staff. In July 1979 a piece called 'The National Trust Navy' appeared in *Harpers & Queen*.[24] This gossip-ridden article described the 'art-historical' industry which has been built up around the preserved country house. As Reyner Banham commented in a withering riposte, the 'Navy' consists of 'roving bands of mansion-fanciers and peerage-buffs who go round invading stately homes . . . for fun and profit in the guise of historical scholarship.'[25] The Navy, as *Harpers & Queen* has ample reason to know, has become a powerful force in the land. In the early days people entered this circle via routes of the traditional Eton and Oxford variety. But things have changed since the days of James Lees-Milne, John Cornforth and John Fowler. By 1967 it had apparently become clear to everyone that machines had 'destroyed the quality of life', and heritage has been booming ever since. The new Navy may affect the old tweediness but, as we are assured, it is no longer a marginal circle of enthusiasts. Finding themselves 'priests of a huge new cult', its members minister to followers who, as the *Harpers* article suggests, owe their historical education to BBC television serials about the Tudors and Edwardians. They come, as often as not, from 'a semi in Bromley', and their careers prove that art history and upward mobility can go happily together. They operate in a healthy market and their knowledge – often far from perfect – is supported by a guidebook carefully hidden in a deep pocket. Like Theo Crosby, the new Navy is said to recognize that Britain is going over to 'service' industries and that tourism is the new infrastructure: 'what could be more of a draw than the stately homes?'

The rebirth of the country house has certainly brought new opportunities for the advocate and commentator. Mark Girouard has shown that books addressed to the new interest can become best-sellers, and employment prospects have improved dramatically as a whole range of new opportunities have opened up: advising television companies on period decor, acting as consultant to upmarket estate agents (Gervase Jackson-Stops, the Trust's architectural adviser, keeps connections with the old family firm of Jackson-Stops and Staff), assisting at the auction houses which are booming now that 'old signed things are important to the economy'. The Lutyens revival of the late 1970s and early 1980s was a Navy promotion, and the present 'classical revival' in architecture has similar connections. There have been related developments in art history with, for example, the elevation of the collector as a focus for art historical study. The polarity between heritage and danger persists throughout, and the advocates of 'heritage' have worked hard to ensure that the encompassing 'danger' is properly identified. By the late 1970s, when Brideshead became a huge television spectacular, an impressive negative imagery of towerblocks, bureaucrats, social workers, inhuman (and foreign) Modernist architects and socialist bulldozers had been built up and placed where those few luxurious 'blocks of flats' had stood in Evelyn Waugh's novel. While the rise of the country house has brought the Navy new opportunities and wider influence, it seems also to have narrowed the range of acceptable political opinion. The Navy speaks for the nation, but its heart is more firmly on the right than ever before. Where the old campaigning groups – from the National Trust through to the Victorian Society and even the

Georgian Group – tried to operate with a broad political
membership, the leading figures of newer organizations like *Save
Britain's Heritage* and the *Thirties Society* share common ground
somewhere between the Conservatism of the *Daily Telegraph* and
that of the *Spectator*.

Meanwhile the interior aesthetic which the Trust has built up
around the preserved country house has also followed an
interesting career through the years of the welfare state. Country
houses have come to the Trust through an arrangement that
guarantees continued rights of residence to the family, and the
chosen style of interior display has always made a special feature
of ancestral continuity. The family itself is incorporated into the
exhibition: its possessions displayed in a vital associational
context which ensures that the whole is always more than the
sum of its parts. The basic features of this interior aesthetic were
outlined early on by Vita Sackville-West, a vigorous pioneer of
the Country Houses Scheme who was busy re-establishing her
own ancestral home and garden at Sissinghurst (recently acquired
in ruinous state as the place where her ancient forebears had
lived) – at the same time as writers like Evelyn Waugh, Osbert
Sitwell and Dornford Yates were fearing the worst. In *English
Country Houses* (1941) Sackville-West, whose house had stood
immediately beneath the Battle of Britain in 1940, admitted the
danger:[26]

> If these English houses of ours were all to be turned into
> institutional buildings, schools, asylums, hotels and the like,
> something of our national heritage of pride and beauty would be
> gone. Museums? A museum is a dead thing; a house which is still
> the home of men and women is a living thing which has not lost
> its soul.

And of what does a house's 'soul' consist?

> I think the characteristic is that the inside has 'grown' in the same
> way as the outside has grown. There is no question of a 'period'
> room, so beloved of professional decorators. Everything is
> muddled up. You may find Jacobean panelling, Chippendale
> tables, Chinoiserie wall-papers, Carolean love seats, Genoa

velvets, Georgian brocades, Burgundian tapestries, Queen Anne embroideries, William and Mary tallboys, Elizabethan bread cupboards, and even Victorian sideboards, all in such a mixture as to make the purist shudder. There was no such thing as a purist period-room decoration. . . . Where is the Dictator of Taste to say who is right and who wrong, what is 'good' and what is 'bad'? All we know is that our ancestors piled up their possessions generation by generation, and somehow managed to create a whole which is far more of a whole than any whole deliberately composed.

Lees-Milne's diaries are full of such interiors. Set off against the public world, the National Trust interior has its own quite unique order of meaning. It is a place of private and incremental meaning, a place of cultural accumulation and a kind of knowledge which stands superior to anything that can be derived from the disciplines of the public museum or academy. Just as John Fowler, the National Trust's favoured 'decorator' from the late 1950s, scorned the idea of 'design', Lees-Milne distinguished the true country house interior from synthetically produced 'period' styles and the 'contrived "old world" flavour' of an architect like Lutyens.[27] In June 1944 James Lees-Milne visited Lord and Lady Braybrooke at Audley End and his description echoes Sackville-West: 'The great hall and the Fish Saloon are very impressive. There is an early nineteenth-century flavour in the paintwork of the rooms. The portrait copies in the Saloon are atrocious. Some Adam suites of furniture are good of their kind, but there is a great deal of indifferent stuff in the rooms, which makes Audley End a true English country house, and not a museum.'[28]

Like other characteristics of the early Country Houses Scheme, this ancestralized interior aesthetic has developed wider resonances in more recent years. Behind the door, which only the Trust can open with proper discretion, lies an esoteric chamber of private association where the centuries are still in place. Preserved against a modern world where history has degenerated into false 'progress', the National Trust interior is one of the few places where the past has been allowed to accumulate undisturbed. Here, priceless masterpieces are mixed up with stuff that would be indistinguishable from ordinary household junk were it not for the enchantment of ancestral association. In the terms developed by Stephen Bann, the National Trust interior is a place of synecdoche rather than metonymy, a place of metaphoric significance where things gain by association and where the whole is indeed always more than the sum of its parts.[29] This interior turned up with new significance at Calke Abbey in 1983. Here, as Marcus Binney put it, was 'the house where time stood still' – a miraculous place which modern history had never reached and where nothing had been thrown away.[30] There was even a drawing room which had been kept shuttered and under wraps since it was redecorated and furnished in 1856. The dustsheets were lifted, the shutters unbarred and folded back just as they had been by Sebastian Flyte at Brideshead, and there – like a glimpse that might be had 'from the top of an omnibus into a lighted ballroom' – was the brilliant world we thought was lost, a perfect television history interior.[31] Some, like Lord John Vaizey (himself busy with the restoration of Cumberland Lodge in Windsor Great Park), thought the heritage lobby was exaggerating the importance of Calke. But where he saw only 'skiploads of junk' (asking 'Is this what is meant by heritage?') others knew true incremental meaning when they saw it and were in no doubt. The house became a symbol of the nation which had survived the dark age of egalitarian reform: a place that deserved to be 'saved' with all the dramatic largesse of a special grant announced in Nigel Lawson's first budget speech. The state was back in safe hands, and the old nation could rest assured.

First defined in the country house, the National Trust's interior aesthetic has since proved itself a movable feast, and started to turn up in altogether less likely places. As the reforming bulldozers grind to a halt in the inner city areas, it has gone on to play a prominent part in the recently defined 'New Georgian' style of gentrification and urban reclamation. Earlier waves of gentrification may have been justified by their claims to upgrade whole areas, but the New Georgians are not interested in uniformity of any sort. What they like is the disparity and contrast of an inner city that has withstood the levelling embrace of the welfare state. The New Georgian ambition is to scoop up the Georgian house which survives in the midst of slum or ghetto, reconstruct it as a private historical world (often without electricity), and then to step out onto the wild side of an unameliorated urban experience. The public street, over which egalitarianism has failed to rule, is returned to its eighteenth-century vocation as a domain of exotic and unpredictable encounter. Inside, meanwhile, the old imagery of slum 'squalor' is also reclaimed from the welfare state which had threatened to finish it off for good, and then authenticated via art history and the importation of culturally resonant clobber. The Bengali sweatshop becomes a valuable early Georgian dwelling again, essays describing the Huguenots as the acceptable kind of immigrant start to appear in the *Spectator*, and the estate agents, quick to put a monetary value on the cultural achievements of these New Georgian pioneers, move in.[32]

But the most telling presentation of the National Trust interior took place when the Trust opened its *Treasure Houses of Britain* exhibition in Washington. Here were the spectacular yields of the Country Houses Scheme organized, consistently enough, as a series of country house interiors. The exhibition placed the private aristocratic past at the centre of its definition of the national culture and was criticized at the time for celebrating the aristocrat as a figure of profound culture and humanity.[33]

The exhibition catalogue, a sumptuous volume of almost unprecedented tonnage, included an essay by Marcus Binney and Gervase Jackson-Stops reviewing 'the last hundred years' of British history from the viewpoint of the country house. As this essay showed, when the country house is taken as the yardstick of national history, every attempt at redistribution and reform looks treasonable: death duties introduced by a Liberal government in 1894, Lloyd George's 'People's Budget' of 1909, Ramsay MacDonald's socialist party which caused the idea of domestic service to be considered 'demeaning'.[34]

The argument about ancestral continuity and the inimitable aura achieved by objects in their proper associational context was also prominently displayed. While the implied criticism of the public museum fits well into an age of cuts, privatization and

admission charges back home, it finds different connections in
the United States where it is used to persuade Americans that
their own well-stocked museums cannot hope to rival the
authenticity of a visit to the old country. This ingenious
application of aesthetics to the promotion of tourism is good
patriotic stuff, but there is more to the catalogue than this.

In his discussion of 'The British as Collectors', Francis Haskell,
Professor of Art History at Oxford University, quotes from
what in the years of the country house aesthetic has indeed
become something of an inaugural moment for the National
Trust. Going back beyond the 1890s, when the Trust was
actually formed, Haskell raised the voice of Quatremère de
Quincy, the French archaeologist and theorist of museums, from
the 1790s. It was then in Paris that the Museum of French
Monuments was established: a public institution set up by the
revolutionary authorities to save valued artefacts from the blows
of over-zealous republicans, and to incorporate them into
programmes of political re-education. As Haskell has described
elsewhere, Chateaubriand and other figures of the Right
condemned this disenchanting (and short-lived) museum as a
wretched attempt to separate art from its proper identity with
Church, Aristocracy and Monarchy.[35] It was in his attack on this
museum that Quatremère de Quincy launched the modern
argument about the vitality of associational context and the
humiliation suffered by works of art when they are exhibited in
statutory public space. There could scarcely be clearer illustration
of the cultural drift which has beset the National Trust since the
Country Houses Scheme was set in train in the 1930s. Set up to
assert a public interest in landscapes and buildings over the
delinquency and neglect of private owners, the post-war country
house aesthetic now offers to refound the organization in the
French 1790s, aligning it with a reactionary assertion of private
meaning, and identifying the public interest with the rampaging
egalitarianism of a demented mob.

Heritage and social polemic

As it has come down to the 1980s, the story of the national
heritage and its preservation is shadowed by the most bitter

social polemic. The conservationist agenda has been over-determined: and not just by rising popularity, television history and the theme-parks of the new leisure industry. I have discussed this with reference to the National Trust's Country Houses Scheme, but the same broader resonances are often to be heard when the 'national heritage' is at issue. They were in the air when the Mary Rose was raised from the mud of the Solent within weeks of the Falklands victory: in both cases the same language of recovery announced that 'we' had regained something which had been lost. They were also to be heard in the recent campaign, launched by the Thirties Society and developed in the pages of the *Spectator*, to preserve the nation's old red telephone boxes. Ostensibly about the architectural superiority of the old Scott kiosks that the newly privatized Telecom wanted to dispose of, this architectural contest touched on broader questions about public service, bureaucracy and the fate of ideas of universal provision in the world of privatized consumer relations. At times the broader social polemic breaks through quite explicitly. It could hardly be missed, for example, in recent disputations between metal detectorists and archaeologists concerned to amend Treasure Trove law. The archaeologists and museum professionals used the vocabulary of 'our threatened national heritage' to condemn the metal detectorists as vandals and land-pirates, but they found themselves caught in a counter-accusation of considerable force: set up as Marxist advocates of state control, they have yet to secure any legislative change at all. An equally open polemic marks the current revival of classical architecture. Quinlan Terry's work is based not just on an apparently fundamentalist idea of the divine origins of the classical orders but also on a detailed rejection of the reforming ambitions of post-war society.[36] Meanwhile Leon Krier, a London-based architect of Belgian extraction who is currently trying to rehabilitate the classical architecture of the Nazi Albert Speer, is animated by an even more vituperative loathing for a post-war spirit which he considers to have declared war on culture and, in a phrase that is reminiscent of Theo Crosby, to have failed to produce 'a single place or monument which a people could long for or dream about'. If Prince Charles said it for the Luftwaffe, Krier (who is included, together with Theo

Crosby, among the Prince's circle of architectural advisers) had already done so for the allied air forces: it was not bombs but the 'moral depravity' of post-war modernism that really put an end to the true German city.[37]

We only have to consider this polemical drama for a moment to recognize that while the opposition between heritage and danger has expressed urgent problems concerning tradition and cultural preservation, it has also been overtaken by a veritable war of the worlds. On the one side stands the endangered old nation: an aristocratic world of private value and hierarchy, where history is associated with tradition and belonging is based on cultural ideas of ancestral descent. On the other is the modern society of post-war reform: a world of public egalitarianism, where history is associated with progress and state-led redevelopment, where belonging follows from citizenship and the political idea of consent. These schematic images of Britain have been defined in polemical opposition to each other since the war. Moreover, the balance between them has changed dramatically. In the 1940s, the traditional nation was crumbling in the shadows of the progressive state. By the end of the 1970s, however, the situation had been reversed. Brideshead was gleaming with restored confidence, while Attlee's utopia was being buried under the negative symbolism of a thousand collapsing tower blocks. Brideshead became a television spectacular in 1981, but it had already been preceded by 'City of Towers', Christopher Booker's devastating documentary on the tower block. It was during this dedication ceremony, in which the much-hated council tower block was declared a monument to Attlee's 1945, that Conservative champions of Brideshead like David Watkin and Roger Scruton rounded on Nikolaus Pevsner, chastising him for his polemical allegiance to Modernism, while brazenly passing off their own polemic (which was in the tradition of James Lees-Milne) as properly disciplined aesthetic truth.[38]

As morbid simplifications, these opposed images of the nation are inadequate to the social complexities which they express. To quote only one example, the 'answer' to the many problems of post-war public housing are scarcely to be found in a return to grand *private* architecture of the sort that Quinlan Terry has developed in polemical response to the modern housing project. It is scarcely surprising in this situation that some critics should have called down a curse on the whole 'heritage industry'. Some have returned, deliberately or not, to the ground sketched out by J. H. Plumb in the 1960s: dismissing 'the past' as delusion, manipulated nostalgia or even 'a created ideology with a purpose', and calling for a return to 'history' as the superior and true form of knowledge which alone can dispel it.[39] Robert Hewison has tried to institute a break between what he calls 'heritage culture' – that regrettable and backward-looking obsession with a fictionalized past – and the superior, but almost entirely unspecified, 'critical culture' that must apparently replace it. It is, of course, easy enough to sneer at the new theme parks, but this response has already started to look like a rehabilitation of old forms of snobbery. Meanwhile, on the other side of the opposition between heritage and danger some critics have tried to contest the identification of Attlee's 1945 with the tower blocks. Prominent among these is Jules Lubbock, who has suggested not only that 'heritage' is an unproblematic term which really belongs to the left, but also that the tower blocks which have been made into such a potent symbol of the 'overweening state' were actually the works of Conservative governments which pressed local authorities to build high.[40]

I'm not convinced by either of these responses. It is certainly true that 'the past' has been conscripted to brazenly political aims and, as Theo Crosby showed us, it is not just old imperial dreams that have been rehabilitated under the name of 'heritage'. 'Heritage' has become the byword for a post-egalitarian modern-ization process which includes what Ralph Lauren calls 'lifestyle marketing' and urban redevelopment. As for the ancestralized country house interior, here the polemical drama has threatened the crudest reduction of all: turning this aesthetic construct into a crude response to post-war immigration. But morbidities of this sort notwithstanding, the post-war rise of the past also testifies to the real dislocation of social memory which has occurred during the years of the welfare state: a dislocation which has followed from the advent of professional planning, the extension of state authority and expertise into new areas of everyday life,

the destruction of traditional patterns of work in the face of
enormous technological change, the loss of traditional 'community' (a value which is still greeted with contempt by many
on the left). Just as it is inadequate to suggest that Labour
governments were entirely innocent of this disruption, it would
also be wrong to dismiss the public sense of history which has
emerged against this background as weak-minded nostalgia.
There are more sufficient ways of thinking about the past and its
rise in this connection with a destabilized social memory. We
might usefully remember Ernst Bloch, the Marxist philosopher
of 'hope' who, in his old age in the 1970s, was defending
'heritage' as the seed of 'hope' to be cherished against the
'polished up death' of a technocratic civilization exemplified by
Modernist architecture.[41] It is here too that we find Walter
Benjamin's defence of nostalgia – his portrayal of people reaching
out to 'seize hold of a memory as it flashes up at a moment of
danger'.[42] When Habermas suggested that tradition has become
the crux of a new tension in modern Western societies, he too
was thinking at the level of social memory. Far from being
concerned about architectural and artistic traditions, his interest
lay in more vernacular customs, habits and ways of life. These
were the traditions that he saw being both eroded and made all
the more necessary by modern developments of capital and state.
A society set on this course would, as he suggested, tend to
destroy the traditions that lent it legitimacy and motivated its
members to participate. Habermas's account of this new
'contradiction' may be overly-schematic, but the tension he is
describing stands squarely behind the post-war drama of
Brideshead and the Tower Blocks.[43]

Meanwhile, the National Trust has recently been coming
under fire from the right. An old ally like *Country Life* has begun
to chide the Trust for behaving as a 'private fiefdom'.[44] James
Lees-Milne has predicted that the country house will soon die of
its own cult, suggesting that in the age of Mark Girouard it has
suffered such over-exposure that boredom is bound to follow.[45]
In 1984 Roger Scruton attacked the Trust's Country Houses
Scheme for 'extinguish[ing] one after another these little fires of
our national inheritance in the ice-cold waters of the bureaucratic

state'.[46] Knowing how much the country house owes to the National Trust, one might suspect a churlish lack of gratitude here. But the truth is that the climate is changing yet again. The new prospect was clearly outlined in 1987 when John Martin Robinson commemorated the fiftieth anniversary of the Country Houses Scheme in the *Spectator*. Full of praise for James Lees-Milne and the organization which had been 'Holding the bridge for fifty years', he signed off with an unmistakable farewell. However sympathetically it is cared for, a country house 'obviously loses its point when it ceases to be the seat of a great county family and becomes merely a museum'. Even with the best will in the world, it is difficult to continue to live in your ancestral home when you are no longer the owner:[47]

> It can be galling to be told that your dinner guests cannot park in the courtyard, or to be charged 6p by the gardener every time you pick a sprig of parsley, or to have a curator, not appointed by yourself, and his mistress, living under the same roof. As a result the younger generation, if not the donors themselves, have tended to move out . . .

The late 1980s offer 'a far more attractive economic climate for private owners' which will ensure that fewer houses will be coming the Trust's way in the future. After the 1988 budget, there will be more people wanting their piece of the heritage back, and the National Trust will have an opportunity to take its concern with the public interest elsewhere. As for James Lees-Milne, A. L. Rowse recently did the decent thing, suggesting that he should be made into an Earl for saving so many great houses from destruction in the 1940s. He added that Lees-Milne had always been hard on the left, and that it really was time to acknowledge how Hugh Dalton, as a minister in the Attlee government and architect of the National Land Fund, 'went out of his way to make generous grants for conservation of country houses, countryside, the nation's inheritance from better days and a more civilised society'.[48] This wouldn't be a bad exchange, but I'm sure it could be improved no end with a bit of help from Theo Crosby. 1945 is suffering terrible neglect in the national memory. Acknowledgement is one thing, but a new monument in Docklands – one very different from that proposed for the Battle of Britain – would surely be better.

Notes

1 Theo Crosby, Pedro Guedes and Michael Sandle, *The Battle of Britain Monument*, London: Pentagram Design Ltd, 1987; and Theo Crosby, *Let's Build a Monument*, London: Pentagram Design Ltd, 1987.
2 These powerful words may not have been any more 'original' than Crosby's own monument. Writing in the 1940s, George Speaight suggested that Churchill drew his rhetoric from the nineteenth-century Toy Theatre plays which were a prominent feature of his childhood. See Speaight, *The History of the English Toy Theatre*, London: Studio Vista, 1969.
3 Martin Pawley, 'Monumental folly', *Designer*, Nov.–Dec. 1987, p. 36. See also Pawley's 'Reaching for the skies', *Guardian*, 8 Sept. 1987.
4 For a useful discussion of the part played by artistic and preserva-tionist values in the redevelopment of loft-space in Lower Manhattan see Sharon Zukin, *Loft-Living: Culture and Capital in Urban Change*, London: Radius, 1988.
5 Umberto Eco, *Travels in Hyper-reality*, London: Picador, 1986. For Jean Baudrillard's spurious reading of the Barbie and Waldheim affairs see 'Hunting Nazis and losing reality', *New Statesman*, 19 Feb. 1988.
6 Derwent May, 'Readers' choice for a plinth', *Sunday Telegraph*, 10 April 1988, p. 26. For Dowding's own interest in the Trafalgar Square plinth see the letter from D. B. Ogilvie in the same issue (p. 11).
7 HRH The Prince of Wales, 'The Mansion House speech', reprinted in *Modern Painters*, 1 (1) (Spring 1988), pp. 29–33.
8 Angela Thirkell, *Peace Breaks Out*, London: Hamish Hamilton, 1946.
9 Harold Speed pleaded the cause of 'real as opposed to abstract art' in *What is the Good of Art?*, London: Allen and Unwin, 1936. This book provides an interesting comparison with more recent defences

of 'real' culture. See, for example, Alan Powers (ed.), *Real Architecture*, London: The Building Centre Trust, 1987.

10 Evelyn Waugh, *Brideshead Revisited*, Harmondsworth: Penguin, 1987. Waugh's Charles Ryder is a country house painter of little talent who owes his overblown reputation to his countrymen's tendency to 'salute their achievements at the moment of extinction'. Robert Hewison uses *Brideshead Revisited* in his recent discussion of the National Trust – see his *The Heritage Industry: Britain in a Climate of Decline*, London: Methuen, 1987. But the connection was made before that by the National Trust's current architectural adviser. See Marcus Binney and Gervase Jackson-Stops, 'The last hundred years', in the catalogue to the Trust's 1985 Washington exhibition, G. Jackson-Stops (ed.), *The Treasure Houses of Britain: Five Hundred Years of Private Patronage and Art Collecting*, New Haven, Conn., and London: Yale University Press, 1985.

11 Osbert Sitwell, Foreword to Ralph Dutton, *The English Country House*, London: Batsford, 1935, p. vi.

12 Dornford Yates, *The House that Berry Built*, London: Ward, Lock & Co., 1945.

13 This Conservative abomination of the professional architect re-appears, strengthened and given a more explicitly anti-modernist turn after the towerblock saga, in the thought of Roger Scruton. See his 'Against architecture', in *Untimely Tracts*, London: Macmillan, 1987, pp. 3–4.

14 Quoted from the cover of James Lees-Milne, *Stourhead: a Property of the National Trust*, London: Country Life, 1948.

15 See Graham Murphy, *Founders of the National Trust*, London: Christopher Helm, 1987, p. 108.

16 James Lees-Milne, 'The country house', in Lees-Milne (ed.), *The National Trust: a Record of Fifty Years' Achievement*, London: Batsford, 1945, p. 61.

17 James Lees-Milne, *Another Self*, London: Faber & Faber, 1984, p. 49.

18 Ibid., pp. 94–5.

19 James Lees-Milne, *Midway on the Waves*, London: Faber & Faber, 1985, p. 29.

20 A letter signed by Lords Esher and Crawford and Balcarres as well as by George Lansbury appeared in *The Times*, 10 Dec. 1936. For a discussion of the more recent trials of Sutton House see my 'Why the blight must be so stark', *Guardian*, 1 Aug. 1987.

21 John Summerson, 'Town buildings', in Lees-Milne (ed.), *The National Trust*, pp. 97–102. Lees-Milne's words on Sutton House

(then known as St. John's Institute) appear in his *Caves of Ice*, London: Faber & Faber, 1984.

22 James Lees-Milne, *The National Trust Guide – Buildings*, London: Batsford, 1948.

23 Robert Hewison, *The Heritage Industry*, pp. 67–8.

24 Gloria Gladstone and Victoria Mather, 'The National Trust Navy', *Harpers & Queen*, July 1979, pp. 84–7 and 174–5. This article written by genuine or pseudonymous Navy members bears more than a passing stylistic resemblance to Alexandra Artley and John Martin Robinson, *The New Georgian Handbook*, London: Ebury Press, 1985.

25 Reyner Banham, 'King Lut's Navy', *New Society*, 12 Nov. 1981, pp. 284–5.

26 V. Sackville-West, *English Country Houses*, London: Collins, 1941, pp. 47 and 30.

27 On John Fowler see John Cornforth, *The Inspiration of the Past: Country House Taste in the Twentieth Century*, Harmondsworth: Viking, 1985. James Lees-Milne is quoted from his *Prophesying Peace*, London: Faber & Faber, 1984, p. 76.

28 *Prophesying Peace*, p. 72.

29 Stephen Bann, *The Clothing of Clio: A Study of the Representation of History in Nineteenth Century Britain and France*, Cambridge University Press, 1984.

30 Marcus Binney, *Our Vanishing Heritage*, London: Arlington Books, 1984, p. 75. Photographs of the newly discovered Calke Abbey appeared in the *Observer Magazine*, 25 March 1984. My own discussion of the Calke episode is in *On Living in an Old Country*, London: Verso, 1985, pp. 38–42.

31 *Brideshead Revisited*, p. 47. Themes from this novel keep reappearing in the writings of the National Trust Navy. Anyone who doubts what the dreadful 'Beryl' might have done to Brideshead had Lord Marchmain not seen her off with a last-minute change in his will should consult Alexandra Artley and Thomas Dibdin's account of Raine Spencer – 'second wife and sharp lady from Haute Suburbia' – and her desecration of Althorpe. See 'Restoration comedy', *Harpers & Queen*, April 1987.

32 Artley and Robinson, *New Georgian Handbook*. My own account of the 'New Georgian' scenario as it was played out in Spitalfields appeared in 'Rodinsky's Place', a review of Ian Sinclair's *White Chappell, Scarlet Tracings*, in *London Review of Books*, 29 Oct. 1987. For Gavin Stamp's description of the Huguenots as immigrants who were 'indistinguishable from the English by colour and race' and,

above all, did nothing to 'offend national sensibilities', see his 'A culture in crisis', *Spectator*, 12 Oct. 1985.

33 Linda Colley, 'The cult of the country house', *Times Literary Supplement*, 15 Nov. 1985. David Cannadine, 'Brideshead re-Revisited', *New York Review of Books*, 19 Dec. 1985.

34 Marcus Binney and Gervase Jackson-Stops, 'The last hundred years', in G. Jackson-Stops (ed.), *The Treasure Houses of Britain: Five Hundred Years of Private Patronage and Art Collecting*, New Haven, Conn., and London: Yale University Press, 1985, pp. 70–8. Lloyd George's 'People's Budget' is still capable of stirring up disputation on the correspondence page of the *Spectator*. The issue of 26 March 1988 included a letter from C. A. Latimer – a self-described Thatcherite – who wrote to contest the idea that the rich had been more generous before 1914. Lloyd George's budget put income tax up from 1s. to 1s.2d. in the pound and the uproar that followed in the House of Lords was intense: 'Anybody would have thought that the world had come to an end.' Latimer was promptly attacked by John Martin Robinson, co-author of the *New Georgian Handbook* and a man whose sense of chronology seems rather awry (even though his sense of history is polemically precise), for favouring governments which 'confiscate' the 'capital and income of private citizens' and fritter it away on 'worthwhile projects like the Blue Streak Rocket, Marsham Street Office Blocks, motorways and the creation of a counter-productive civil service bureaucracy on the scale of Tsarist Russia' (2 April 1988). C. A. Latimer, who replied on 16 April 1988, is clearly not *au fait* with this new way of understanding Lloyd George's pension scheme which, as he pointed out helplessly, had surely been modest enough, offering '5s a week if you lived to be 70, and 7s.6d. for a married couple'.

35 Francis Haskell, 'The British as collectors', in *The Treasure Houses of Britain*, pp. 50–60. See also Haskell's 'Les musées et leurs ennemis', *Actes de la Recherche en science sociales*, 49 (1983), pp. 103–6.

36 I have discussed these examples more fully elsewhere: the Mary Rose in *On Living in an Old Country*, pp. 161–92; the telephone box in 'A symbol of national embarrassment', *The Listener*, 15 Oct. 1980, pp. 17–18; metal detectorists in 'Treasure Island', *New Society*, 21 Aug. 1987, pp. 14–17; Quinlan Terry in 'Ideal homes', *New Socialist*, Oct. 1985, pp. 16–21.

37 Leon Krier, 'An architecture of desire', in Krier (ed.), *Albert Speer: Architecture 1932–42*, Brussels: Archives d'Architecture Moderne, 1985.

38 The key book here was David Watkin, *Morality and Architecture*, Chicago and London: University of Chicago Press, 1977. As the author of this study, Watkin is certainly the man to recognize that 'the Modern Movement . . . was like a giant act of political nationalisation, and its break-up is a process curiously akin to the rhetorical emphases on freedom of choice and privatisation which characterise Mrs. Thatcher's Britain.' (Quoted from Watkin's review of J. Mordaunt Crook, *The Dilemma of Style: Architectural Ideas from the Picturesque to the Post-Modern*, in *Landscape*, Feb. 1988, pp. 87–9.)

39 J. H. Plumb, *The Death of the Past*, London: Macmillan, 1969, p. 17.

40 Jules Lubbock tries to clear the left of any responsibility for post-war high-rise redevelopment in 'Building blocks', an interview published in *Marxism Today*, March 1988, pp. 40–1.

41 Ernst Bloch, 'Building in empty spaces', in *The Utopian Function of Art and Literature*, Cambridge, Mass., and London: MIT Press, 1988, pp. 186–99.

42 Walter Benjamin, 'Theses on the philosophy of history', in *Illuminations*, London: Fontana, 1973, p. 257.

43 Jurgen Habermas, *Legitimation Crisis*, London: Heinemann, 1976.

44 Michael Hanson, 'Trust the National Trust', *Country Life*, 16 July 1987.

45 James Lees-Milne, review of Mark Girouard's *A Country House Companion*, in the *Spectator*, 28 Nov. 1987, pp. 45–6.

46 Roger Scruton, 'The stately and the state-controlled', in *Untimely Tracts*, London: Macmillan, 1987, p. 115.

47 John Martin Robinson, 'Holding the bridge for fifty years', the *Spectator*, 18 April 1987, pp. 35–6.

48 A. L. Rowse, review of Lees-Milne's *Caves of Ice*, in the *Spectator*, 22 Feb. 1983, p. 22.

Since writing this article I have met James Lees-Milne and found his contemporary views every bit as interesting as those he held as a young man. He defended the National Trust against the bullish right-wing privateers, who are now talking as though the Country Houses Scheme had done nothing more than expropriate the homes of the aristocracy. He also called Attlee a 'saint' of a kind, remarking that in his experience Labour governments had always done more for conservation than their Conservative counterparts. See my 'James Lees-Milne, a superannuated man?', in *Modern Painters*, 5, Spring 1989.

Contributors

THOMAS BUTLER   Slavonic philologist and translator. Visiting Pro-
fessor at Boston College, 1988–9; Charter Fellow, Wolfson College,
University of Oxford, 1986–7, and Visiting Fellow, 1987–8.
Professor Butler holds a Ph.D. from Harvard University. He has
taught Slavonic languages and literatures at the universities of
Harvard, Oxford and Wisconsin, and at Tufts. Recipient of a
National Endowment for the Humanities Fellowship for translation
(1983–4), he has translated from a variety of Slavonic languages. His
*Monumenta Serbocroatica: A Bilingual Anthology of Serbian and Croatian
Texts* (1980) was chosen as a 'book of the year' by *Quest*, the journal
of the American Library Association. He has twice been selected
Fulbright Senior Research Professor in Yugoslavia.

ALAN D. BADDELEY   Psychologist, University of Cambridge;
Director of the MRC Applied Psychology Unit, Cambridge. He
holds degrees from University College London (BA), Princeton
University (MA), and the University of Cambridge (Ph.D.). He has
taught at the universities of Sussex and Stirling, Scotland. Dr
Baddeley has written extensively on memory. His most recent books
are *Working Memory* (1986) and *Your Memory: A User's Guide* (1982).
He is Chairman of the Board of the European Society for Cognitive
Psychology, as well as Chairman of the Medical Research Council
Neurosciences Board. He is a member of the editorial boards of
several journals of cognitive psychology.

BANI SHORTER   Jungian analyst and author, London. She holds the
Dipl. Analyt. Psych. from the C. G. Jung Institute, Zurich. She has
published *An Image Darkly Forming: Women and Initiation* (1987) and is
co-author with Andrew Samuels and Fred Plaut of *A Critical
Dictionary of Jungian Analysis* (1986). She lectures widely in the UK

and abroad, and has served as Chairman of the Guild of Pastoral Psychology, London. She is a founder-member of the Independent Group of Analytical Psychologists and was its first Coordinator of Preparation for those becoming analysts.

KRINKA VIDAKOVIĆ PETROV Dr Petrov studied at the universities of Belgrade (BA, MA) and Zagreb (Ph.D. 1982) and is a Research Associate of the Institute for Literature and Art, Belgrade. She has written numerous articles on Sephardic, Serbo-Croatian and Spanish folklore, as well as on Latin American literature, and is the author of *The Culture of Spanish Jews on Yugoslav Soil* (Sarajevo, 1986). Dr Petrov has translated works by Borges and García Márquez, among others. She has taught Serbo-Croatian at Indiana, Kansas, and Ohio State universities.

PETER BURKE Reader in Cultural History, University of Cambridge, and Fellow of Emmanuel College since 1979. He is author of *The Renaissance Sense of the Past* (1969) and *Culture and Society in Renaissance Italy* (1972). He has also written *Venice and Amsterdam, A Study of Seventeenth Century Elites* (1974), and *Popular Culture in Early Modern Europe* (1978). His books have been translated into Italian, German, Swedish, Dutch, Spanish, Portuguese and Japanese. He has been Herodotus Fellow at the Institute for Advanced Studies, Princeton; Directeur d'Etudes Associé at the Ecole des Hautes Etudes (Paris); and Visiting Professor at the University of São Paulo.

GEOFFREY A. HOSKING Professor of Russian History, School of Slavonic and East European Studies, University of London. He is author of *The Russian Constitutional Experiment: Government and Duma, 1907–1914* (1973); *Beyond Socialist Realism: Soviet Fiction since Ivan Denisovich* (1980); and *A History of the Soviet Union* (1985). He gave the 1988 series of Reith Lectures for the BBC. Professor Hosking studied at King's College, Cambridge, Moscow State University, and St. Antony's College, Oxford. His Ph.D. is from Cambridge. He has lectured at the universities of Essex, Wisconsin (Visiting Lecturer) and Cologne.

JON STALLWORTHY Reader in English Literature and Fellow of Wolfson College, University of Oxford, since 1986. He is a former Deputy Academic Publisher of Oxford University Press, and was John Wendell Anderson Professor of English Literature at Cornell University, 1977–86. He has published eight collections of poems, most recent of which are: *The Apple Barrel: Selected Poems, 1955–63*

(1974); *Hand in Hand* (1974); *A Familiar Tree* (1978); *The Anzac Sonata: New and Selected Poems* (1986). He has written *Between the Lines: W. B. Yeats's Poetry in the Making* (1963); *Vision and Revision in Yeats's Last Poems* (1969); and also a biography, *Wilfred Owen* (1974, winner of the Duff Cooper Memorial Prize, W. H. Smith Literary Award, and E. M. Forster Award). He has published (with others) several books of translations from Russian and Polish, and is the editor of *The Penguin Book of Love Poetry* (1973); and *Wilfred Owen: Complete Poems and Fragments* (1983); and *The Oxford Book of War Poetry* (1984).

PATRICK WRIGHT   Writer and lecturer. He has worked in the UK, USA and Canada, and is the author of *On Living in an Old Country: The National Past in Contemporary Britain* (1985). Mr Wright is a frequent contributor to the *London Review of Books*, among other journals and newspapers. He has written several radio and television documentaries on subjects concerned with heritage policy. He completed a lecture tour of the Eastern United States in 1987.

Index